Honey, Grain, and Gold
A Devotional for Frey

Joshua Tenpenny

Honey, Grain, and Gold

A Devotional for Frey

edited by

Joshua Tenpenny

Hubbardston, Massachusetts

Asphodel Press
12 Simond Hill Road
Hubbardston, MA 01452

Honey, Grain, and Gold: A Devotional for Frey
© 2010 by Joshua Tenpenny
ISBN 978-0-9825798-2-4

Printed in cooperation with
Lulu Enterprises, Inc.
860 Aviation Parkway, Suite 300
Morrisville, NC 27560

For all you have given me.

Contents

Foreword

Love for the gods can motivate us to do things we never imagined doing, and putting this book together is one of those things. It has been an honor and privilege to assemble this anthology, and the experience has brought me from quietly thinking Frey is really great to confidently identifying as a Freysman. I've shied away from the Northern Tradition for years. As someone who is a peacemaking, service-oriented "light-bringer", I was unable to relate to the conservative, manly warrior virtues of the Asatru, and felt very alone among the radical boundary-pushing ordeal-focused Rökkatru folks. "Love All, Serve All" isn't a motto that gets you much of a place at either table. It is my love of Frey alone that brings me to this project, not my support for any group or movement. I am a devoutly and passionately religious person, an animist and polytheist to the bone, but I'm no more a Heathen than I am a Hindu.

Love is a repeating theme in this book, and Frey being Frey, that love is sometimes expressed through the body. A number of contributions to this book (including one of mine) emphasize the sexual aspect of Frey, and some of those are homoerotic. Because I know the sexual component is off-putting to many people, at times I've wrestled with how far to go with that. Despite being a gay man, I do not always think of Frey in erotic terms. My experience of Frey is primarily one of deep and overwhelming love, a love that makes sexual desire seem trivial ... but still, in spite of this, the metaphors that come to mind when describing this love are sometimes erotic. In any case, sexuality is one way in which Frey relates to his people, and needs to be included here. If this troubles you, I apologize, and I encourage you to skip the third chapter. There is so much more to Frey than sex.

The other repeating theme is food. Hexagram 27 of the *I Ching* says that if we wish to know what someone values, we need only look to see what they choose to nourish themselves. In light of that, all profits for this book go to the Northeast Organic Farming

Association (NOFA), an organization which I respect greatly. I thank Julie Rawson of NOFA and Many Hands Organic Farm for giving me my first experience of organic agriculture on a (small) commercial scale, and who (lovingly but firmly) challenged me on my priorities with regard to the place of organic livestock feed in my household budget.

I thank all of my contributors for putting their experiences, devotion, and love of Frey into words and sharing those words with the world. I thank Elizabeth Vongvisith, who walks the *bhakti* path with me. I thank Kojka, the best doggie ever, who opened my heart to the experience of companion animals. I thank Raven Kaldera, who has taught me so much about love, the gods, and myself, and who has brought me closer to Frey than anyone else possibly could.

But I am also deeply indebted to a very special Freyswoman who will always have a place in my heart. Without you, this book never would have happened. Bless you.

JOSHUA TENPENNY
JUNE 13, 2010

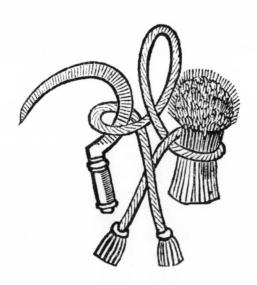

A Note About Rituals And Recipes
Raven Kaldera

The rituals and recipes that end each chapter are not reconstructionist in any way. They are based on the eight astronomical high holidays, some of which the Norse people celebrated, others of which the Anglo-Saxon people celebrated, but none of which have surviving ritual details. These rites are created for Pagans who want to celebrate Frey at any time during the year—as solitary ritual, as a family or household, as a group. They are seasonal and geared to the Wheel of the Year in New England, which means that they may need to be adjusted for people who live in other climates. Feel free to adapt as you like.

Some personal gnosis uncovered by several of the people who contributed to this book indicates that Frey, Freya, and Njord each spend a third of the year in Asgard as hostages. In Frey's case, since he also has a title in Alfheim as the Aesir representative there, he spends a third of the year there as well. This divides his year into three parts. As far as those of us who have seen these visions can tell, he arrives in Vanaheim just before the Summer Solstice, in order to consummate a particular rite with his sister Freya in order to bring fertility to the fields. He stays through Lammas, and his fateful yearly sacrifice, after which he returns. (Some say that he returns to life after a few days and then consummates his marriage again with his wife Gerda, others say that he stays underground, or in the underworld, until the Spring. Our rituals here revolve around the first assumption.) At Samhain, he is feasted as the Harvest King and greets his father Njord coming from Asgard, as he takes his household and relocates to beautiful Alfheim to spend the winter in the land of dreams. In the early spring, he and his wife part; he goes to Asgard, where she will no longer set foot, and she goes back to Jotunheim to her father's hall.

This cycle is interlocked with another cycle, which is that of the turning of the seasons. Thus Frey's year is celebrated by his travels and his passage from one state to another—life to death to life, conjugal to solitary to conjugal, Vanaheim to Alfheim to Asgard. The rituals herein help practitioners to connect with the deep mysteries of his sacred cycles, as well as the experience of his divine life. While this is not documented in any historical source, we have found it to have great meaning for us.

Similarly, the recipes are not meant to be historically period food accurate to the Iron Age or earlier. We know that the ancient Norse and Germanic peoples did not have potatoes or chocolate. But Frey feasts are about seasonal eating, and while the fresh and dried ingredients in these foods are seasonal for our farm in New England, people in other climates may find that other foods are more appropriate at different times. Although creating period food is fun and impressive, we believe that Frey wants to see responsible use of food and agriculture more than he wants to see a particular period recreated. So while we offer these recipes as inspiration, do look to see what is in season in your local area, and try to buy from local growers, including small family farms that need all the help they can get. We especially encourage this with regard to the pig meat that is in so many of these recipes. Pigs, as livestock, have a high rate of requiring constant antibiotics in order to survive in crowded factory-farm conditions. This means that organic, cruelty-free pork is far different from factory pork. Bother to find it, perhaps buying it directly from local organic farmers. Frey understands sacrifice, but he does not want to see more suffering than necessary.

A Note on Orthography

Joshua Tenpenny

When using words from Anglo-Saxon or Old Norse, most of our contributors have used the modern Anglicized forms, which drop ligatures, accent marks, and grammatical features not found in English. A few contributors have retained the original form of some words, and I have chosen to leave these in the form preferred by the author of each piece. However, I'd like to address the two points most likely to cause confusion among people unfamiliar with these languages.

First, in Old Norse, the letters ð and þ are both pronounced approximately like the English "th", with ð being more like the "th" of "there" and þ being more like "thin". In Anglo-Saxon, the distinction is more complex. The exact pronunciation of these, as well as the various accented and unaccented vowels and ligatures, is beyond the scope of this small note.

Second, the name "Frey" is sometimes spelled "Freyr" or "FreyR". These are usually pronounced by English speakers as rhyming with either "mayor" or "fair", or something in between. In Old Norse, a final *r* is often (but not always) a grammatical ending marking the nominative case. So for instance, a word may have a final *r* when it is the subject of a sentence, but not when it is the object. Grammatical endings of this sort are generally dropped when the words are used in English, but some people prefer to keep them.

Son of Vanaheim

Prayer for the Son of Vanaheim
Ari

Hail, Frey the Prince of Vanir soil,
Meeting of the sea and earth,
Son of Njord that floats the ships,
Son of She who gave you birth.

Hail, Frey the Good and Loving Son,
At home in realms both blue and green,
The link between opposing forces,
The cord of love that binds between.

Hail, Frey the fertile Lord of Food,
The fish head buried in the soil
That brings the corn to greater heights,
Hail Frey who blesses honest toil.

Hail, Frey the Golden Child that rode
On Njord's fine decks, in Nerthus's arms,
Whose smile lit up the Vanic morn,
Who smiling blessed the humblest farm.

Honey, Grain, and Gold: Three Aspects of Frey
Jack Roe

> *Green his eyes as garden's yield,*
> *Gold his hair as blowing field,*
> *Bright his laugh as summer's lands,*
> *Brave his heart and empty hands.*

Honey, grain, and gold. These three substances, to me, define Frey's faces and attributes to the world. One could also call them Love, Sacrifice, and Light ... or Sex, Food, and Magic, if you prefer the more straightforward. They are all so beautiful, and all valuable. There's a reason why they are intertwined.

> *Honey on the fingertip,*
> *Gold to pass from hand to lip.*
> *Food of flower, toil of hives,*
> *Work of all the tiny lives.*

The first aspect of Frey that I encountered was that of Frey, the God of Love. People talk a lot about Love Goddesses, but they never mention Love Gods (with the possible exception of arrow-flinging Eros and the Hindu Krishna). Lust Gods, yes. Lots of those, with huge phalluses, flinging themselves onto anything that passed. Emblematic of the overriding sexual urge, said scholars. When I first saw a figure of Frey, it was the one with the enormous cock, and of course I thought that he would be just another sexually aggressive figure. I was surprised to find out, later, that the huge-cocked god of the Germanic peoples was actually gentle, light-bringing, open to sacrifice. In my ignorance, I thought that given the macho-warrior depiction of their culture, that any god with a dick that size was going to have to be a rapist ... yet Frey is the God who gives up his (phallic symbol) sword for Love. He goes to his beloved, without whom the world is not worth living for him, with no aggression in him.

Frey, like his sister, has many ephemeral encounters with both women and men, indiscriminately. At the same time, however, he is indelibly married to Gerda, his giantess-bride. This is unlike Freya, who apparently did get married once but her husband went away and never came back. It is almost as if she is so much more tied to the ephemerality of love that any permanent marriage was doomed; no man could keep that much of her. One is reminded of Venus and Adonis, or Ishtar and Tammuz. On the other hand, Frey's marriage is as solid as the earth beneath him, yet he can still give himself in ephemeral moments of pleasure. Frey and Gerda reliefs were apparently given out as wedding charms, so Frey is as much a god of the marriage bed as of the Maypole festivals. He is the male sexual and emotional responses at their most broad, able to do both roles cleanly and bring only joy.

Honey has been a symbol for love deities in many different cultures. It is the sexual fluids of flowers, it is sweet, it is the color of the sun that warms. From Aphrodite to Oshun, honey or its derivatives were offered to the Ladies of Love. (Mead, however, became an all-around offering to any god in the northlands.) According to legend, Frey is served by an elven couple, one of whom is named Beyla, or Bee. She is Frey's Beekeeper, the provider of his sacred honey, fluid of love.

> *Grain that waves and falls and feeds,*
> *Scythed and ground for hunger's needs,*
> *Blood and steel upon the sheaf,*
> *Praise and revere each gathered leaf.*

Frey's most well-known role is that of a god of food. He is one of the most physically-centered gods I know—sex and food, what can I say? The two most powerful urges in human nature. He is known as the God of the World, in the sense of the physical world that nourishes us, the world of the body. He is the soul of the plants and animals that die to feed us, a mystery that modern humans miss and would do well to turn to again. How would the modern chain of food production change if we revered the taking of all life for food, plant and animal, as a sacred act? We don't think about food or where it came from, and this is one of the great sins in our culture.

Frey's other servant is Byggvir, Beyla's husband, who is his miller for his sacred grain. Honey and grain, sweetener and malt, are also simple components for beer, along with yeast. Like all the Vanir, he is not a god of wilderness. As Kerenyi said of Demeter, he is a "deity of all that is grown for the benefit of mankind". Frey as Grain God is God of contentment, keeping our bellies full and our relaxation moments pleasurable. He is also the Sacrificed One who willingly gives himself for our survival, over and over. One thinks of a sacrificial God as being a solemn thing, yet he is golden and laughing to the end. This is also reflected in his sexuality; he goes to every encounter with a smile and open arms, even if it will end in his death. If you don't want him, he simply doesn't come.

I remember how, decades ago at a Pagan gathering, a man talked about how he saw the male version of the Triple Goddess—maiden, mother, crone—in his own genitals. He spoke of the first ephemeral stirrings of erection as the dallying Green Man, playful rather than serious; the full erection that gives its all in a great spurt was the Corn King, or Sun King at his height, giving everything for life. The limp, withered, wrinkled, quiescent flesh afterwards was the Sage, or Wise Man, whom he hoped someday to be. When I learned about Frey many years later, I remembered this parable of the erection. It isn't that the aggressive phallus isn't a part of male sexuality—it is; the assaultive Gods are part and parcel of the ambivalent package that is testosterone-based sex (and I would point out that female sexuality also has differing and ambivalent parts to it, all of which are true and sacred in their own way), but it is not the only possibility, nor the only thing going on. Frey's sexuality is another aspect of male sexuality, enthusiastic and giving, willing to be the phallus-as-vulnerable. He is the bread marked with the rune of sacrifice, to remind us all. Of the Futhark runes, although many are associated with different Gods, only two actually bear the names of Gods themselves—Teiwaz and Inguz, Tyr and Frey. In a sense, these represent the two contrasting sides of male sexuality—the warrior, whose aggression is controlled only by his honor, and the giving Grain God.

> *Yearly yet his glory fell,*
> *Dark he walks the road to Hel,*
> *Open gate and leave one spark,*
> *Touch of gold in endless dark.*

Golden One. Frey is a light-bringer, and that is one of his mysteries. He is not the Sun itself—that's Sunna/Sol—but he is, as someone once eloquently put it, "the one who guides the rays of light to the leaves of the growing plant." Sunna shines down on everyone and everything indiscriminately, and while she can be benevolent, it's not her job to make sure that everything gets its share of growth-producing rays. When the sunlight comes within reach of the Earth, in a place where food-producing plants or animals live, it becomes Frey's. He captures that golden light and infuses our crops with it, and our animals, and our bodies.

Frey is sacrificed every year and walks the Hel Road, but instead of staying, he is turned away and comes back—some say in three days, some claim it takes months and see him slowly making his way back up through the soil during the dark time of the year. He is the light that descends to the darkness and rises again. Gold, the metal of the Sun, is also his. His sister Freya loves amber, which is said to be her solidified tears, and so does Frey, but as someone I know put it, "Frey likes gold and amber, Freya likes amber and gold."

This is Frey as Sacred King. While we think of Odin as the All-Father of Asgard, and Njord as the King of the Vanir, Frey's kingship is of the other sort. It recalls the stories of the political Kings who didn't want to give up their thrones and be sacrificed after seven years, so they chose someone else to take care of that part of the Kingship for them. Frey is Sacred King as Golden One, he who dies and arises in triumph, not to rule politically but to inspire gloriously. I've always felt that the golden torc was his symbol here, of the earthly (meaning of the Earth itself, not the society of people who live on it) kingship. His connection with Freya shows through here; the Sacred Twins were linked with land rulership in Indo-European tradition.

Frey is the spark of light that survives the Underworld, survives sorrow and loss, and can inspire one not necessarily to great deeds—that's more Odin's work—but to go on living in the face of all despair. That's his greatest gift. When one is in such a bad place that even getting out of bed is an ambivalent option, Frey is the voice that coaxes you to get up, make yourself breakfast, eat it, wash your body, care for your flesh. He reminds us that there is still a little joy to be had in life, somewhere, if we just hold on and keep living.

When the Reformation broke apart western Christianity into Catholic and Protestant, one of the pivotal arguments was transubstantiation—whether the bread and wine given out during the Mass magically and literally became the Body and Blood of Christ through some act of divine magic, or whether it was all just symbolic. In the Mass itself, we see the echoes of an ancient ritual honoring the original Sacrificed Gods, who were Gods of earth and field and grain and grape, borrowed for the Christian's Sacrificed God. With Gods like Frey, such communion is obvious. There's no contradiction; it is both symbolic and quite literally the flesh of the Grain God. I expect that the stain of Christianity has ruined the concept of such a communion ritual for Pagans, which is really too bad. I can imagine such a thing done with Frey's loaves marked with the Inguz rune and spread with honey, tiny sips of some liquor like Goldschlager or, for the less profligate, cups of beer or mead. I would kneel for such communion, and find no contradiction at all.

> *Wooden bowl and wooden cup,*
> *Pour the gold and drink it up,*
> *Taste the gold that Joy can give,*
> *We need no other gold to live.*

The Golden Year
Shannon Graves

Oak Tree Moon
The twins entwine their limbs
in the circle of fruiting trees
as the sun rises, as the earth splits open
the land is blessed and renewed.

Holly Tree Moon
The stallion bears him through the village,
the people strain to touch his feet
and hair as he dismounts to kiss
the women who wail for their wombs to fill.

Hazel Tree Moon
He goes among the men. No women dare watch.
They touch and laugh, hand to staff,
they feed the soil and each other's hungers,
and learn the nature of the turning year.

Grapevine Moon
He is slain in silence. No more is said.
He travels to the dark place and returns,
his wife greets him, bleeding as he bleeds,
their joining is a spell of frith.

Ivy Moon
They are newlyweds always, trembling fingers
that wipe honey on each other's lips,
their love sees beauty in the turning leaves
and surrenders to the autumn forest.

Reed Moon
The Harvest King, he sits enthroned
surrounded by the baskets of bounty,
fruit and nuts and rune-marked loaves
that gleam beneath the twig-struck moon.

Elder Tree Moon
His father's son, he passes him
as they trade places on the wintering shore.
With miller and beekeeper, with wife and friend
he moves the household to the Elven lands.

Birch Tree Moon
The elves feast him in their halls
as his lady keeps her counsel at home
under quilts of old dreams stitched together
he is drunk on faery ale, she opens her arms to him.

Rowan Tree Moon
In the land of glamours he holds court
his tooth-gift, the watchdog of Odin.
He lays with faery maids and laughs
their glamour does not touch him.

Ash Tree Moon
They part with tears, he turns to go
back to Asgard's halls, she goes home
to giant's lands where cold her garden grows.
Crows carry their love-notes, each to each.

Alder Tree Moon
He walks his sister's realm
as she walks their homeland's fields
in returning spring, he feasts with gods
of sky and cloud, and all love him.

Hawthorn Tree Month

Thorns prick deep as he yearns for his love
but still he drowns his sorrow in mead
goes to councils of the mighty ones
and pleads for peace among warriors.

Willow Tree Month

The summer days are gaining hours
as he takes ship at his father's Asgard hall
to see his green homeland once again
to death, to love, to all that moves the worlds.

Invocation to Frey

From the Book of Hours *of the Order of the Horae*

Hail Frey, Lord of the fields!
Lord of the Vanir,
Golden of hair as the fields of wheat,
Bringing riches of heart and hearth
To noble and common folk alike,
We hail you with the corn that springs forth
And falls again to nourish us.
We hail you, mighty boar in flight,
Lord of the phallus that gives life,
Lord of Love that is bound to land,
Love that is bound with commitment,
Love that does not come easily,
As one must toil for the harvest.
Teach us that love is worth working for,
And that work is worth loving,
And that neither lives long without the other.
Lord Frey, Corn God,
Husband of Gerda the etin-bride,
You who can warm the cold heart,
Warrior without a weapon
Who gave your sword for love,
You who make the grain spring forth,
Show us faith in every springtime.

This God Called Frey
Sophie Reicher

Ingvi-Frey is a very popular God within the contemporary Northern Tradition. One of the Vanir, he is commonly associated with fertility, wealth, and peace. According to both the *Gylfaginning* and the *Skaldskaparmal,* Freyr is the Son of Njord, the son of Nerthus, the Brother of Freya, and Kinsman of the Vanir. He is associated not only with wealth and fertility, but also good weather, fruitfulness of the earth, and, as already noted, peace and prosperity. Heathen author Galina Krasskova also associates him with ancestral might and the health of one's community. This latter assertion comes from the belief that Frey fathered a line of kings and as such is a tribal god, but that is something that we will discuss below (Krasskova, p. 89). It's clear that Frey's functions and associations were not only multi-faceted but lay in areas of direct importance to the communities in which he would have been honored.

We don't know very much about the origins of Frey's worship. Accounts of the worship of his mother Nerthus date at least as far back as Roman times, because we know that Tacitus wrote about it in *Germania* in the first century. In *Germania,* he recounts a sacred procession, with the image of the Goddess being carried in a cart, or wain. Later, in the *Ynglinga Saga,* we read of the same practices having been incorporated into common ritual worship of Frey. Some scholars speculate that his worship began in Sweden and from there moved across the continent and onward to Iceland. Certainly there are numerous place names bearing some form of the word "Frey". Such linguistic evidence shows that his worship was most common in Sweden, though it was also found in Norway, Iceland, and elsewhere on the continent (Turville-Petre, p. 168). He even shows up in England, being mentioned the Anglo-Saxon rune poem for Inguz as a God of the harvest:

Ing wæs ærest mid East-Denum
gesewen secgun, oþ he siððan est

ofer wæg gewat; wæn æfter ran;
ðus Heardingas ðone hæle nemdun.

Ing was first seen by men among the East-Danes,
till, followed by his chariot,
he departed eastwards over the waves.
So the Heardingas named the hero.
(http://www.ragweedforge.com/rpae.html)

Ironically for this most popular of Gods, we don't even really know his name. Frey simply means "Lord" as Freya means "Lady". Many Frey's folk that I know speculate that His real name is "Ing" or "Ingvi" but as of now, from the standpoint of certain scholarship, we will probably never know. Ann Groa Sheffield does offer a list of historically accurate by names or *heiti* in her wonderful book, *Frey, God of the World,* which give tantalizing insight into his importance in common worship.

Many scholars believe that the Vanir Gods were an earlier pantheon of Gods, displaced by the Aesir. Certainly relations between the two tribes in Norse lore were not always friendly. The lore tells us that at one time, the two families of Gods were at war. Since both were powerful and relatively equally matched, neither side could win and an uneasy détente was reached. Peace was sealed when the leader of Vanaheim (Njord) agreed to live amongst the Aesir as a hostage to peace along with his son Frey. Freya came as well so as not to be separated from her brother. In addition to splitting his time between Vanaheim and Asgard, Frey has ties to Alfheim in that this world was "gifted" to him as a tooth-gift (Ellis-Davidson, p. 107). Gifted by whom and on what authority, the lore simply doesn't say. Additionally, Frey has some tenuous connections to Jotunheim because he married a mighty giantess, Gerd. Their courtship is told in the Eddic Lay called the *Skirnismal.*

In addition to his associations with fertility, or perhaps as an extension of that function, Frey is sometimes associated with the concept of divine kingship. It is in his role as royal ancestor (the

Ynglinga Saga tells of how he fathered the royal line of Sweden) that we see aspects of yet another function: God of the Barrow-Mound, of the male dead (Ellis-Davidson, p. 154). This is particularly interesting from a linguistic standpoint. The word *alf* can refer to one of the *Alfar*, the inhabitants of Alfheim (commonly anglicized into elf a la Tolkien), but it can also be used to refer to a male ancestor. (The female ancestors are called the *Disir*; singular, *Dis*). It might be interesting to speculate on whether or not the gift of "Alfheim" was not the world of Ljossalfheim, but rather the barrow mound, the smaller "world" of the male dead, or of those sacred places by which the dead can more easily communicate with the living.

As a god of kingship, Frey would have sovereignty over the land. The health of the land traditionally depended upon the health of the king. That is the definition of sacral kingship. Tangential to this function was Frey's role as a God of good seasons (*ár*) and inviolable peace *(frið)*. This, by the way, is the origin for the salute: *til ár ok friðr*. It is a wish for peace and good harvest: abundance, security, and plenty and it stems from this ancient connection between Frey and the land (Sheffield, p. 14-15; Simek also talks about this briefly in his discussion of sacrifice). Of course, the most common view of Frey also includes honoring him as a god of sexuality. Much of his surviving iconography shows him with an erect phallus, as a nod toward his connection to all forms of fecundity and pleasure.

Because of his connection to *frið,* common Heathen ritual practice states that no weapon may be brought into an enclosure sacred to the god Frey. This has strong foundations in the surviving lore. Tacitus notes that as far back as 98 C.E., weapons would not be brought into groves sacred to Nerthus. In the Skirnismal, Frey sacrificed his sword to win the hand of Gerd. This means, incidentally, that at Ragnarok, Frey is the only God who fights unarmed, save for a deer antler. He succeeds in killing his brother-in-law, the giant Beli, ostensibly in this way (thus earning the by-name Beli's Bane). While he may be a god of peace, he obviously was battle-worthy enough not only to win the hand of a mighty giantess, but to fight boldly and bravely *without a weapon*. If he is a god of the earth, then it follows that would encompass not only the fruitful flowering of the land, but the violence and power of the earthquake, volcano, flood, and storm too. Many contemporary priests and priestesses of Frey interpret all of this to mean that they are tabooed from carrying weapons, and will go unarmed (unlike those dedicated to more obviously aggressive Deities).

Touching again on his role as a God of sexuality, Adam of Bremen wrote that Frey was associated with sexual pleasure and that his cultic statue at the great temple in Uppsala showed him with a giant phallus (Adam of Bremen, *Gesta Hammaburgensis ecclesiae pontificum,* book 4, sections 26-27). Ironically for a god of sexuality and fecundity, Frey does not have children. The modern text *Jotunbok,* compiled by Raven Kaldera, discusses why this might be and connects it to Gerda's position amongst the Jotunfolk and Frey's debt to the Aesir. Why would a giantess, after all, wish to raise children who would be bound at least half a year to a race (the Aesir) who despised her own? Some scholars might dispute this, however, noting in Norse mythology the Danish King Fjolnir was said to be the son of Frey and Gerda (see *Ynglinga Saga* and *Grottasöngr).*

If the question of children is unanswered, we do know something of Frey's associates. In addition to his wife Gerd, father Njord and mother Nerthus, his sister Freya is one of the most popular Goddesses in Heathenry: She too is associated with wealth and sexual pleasure. He has a number of servants and aides listed in the surviving lore. There is the Alfar man Skirnir, who functions as Frey's *factotum* and who actually negotiated the courtship between Frey and Gerda. There are his servants Byggvir and his wife Beyla. According to Simek, both may be viewed as protective spirits. He associates Beyla with the cow and thus as protectress of dairy work. Other scholars associate the name etymologically with beans or with bees (Simek, p.36). The bee would be an interesting symbol from a folkloric standpoint, as they have always had strong folkloric associations with healing and magic. Byggvir's name is usually taken etymologically to mean "corn". Simek again ties this tangentially into the Anglo-Saxon story of Scyld Scefing and speculates that it points to a field cult (Simek, p. 50). Frey also has a golden boar named Gullinbursti. The boar was a symbol of abundance and prosperity. Freya is also associated with the Sow for many of the same reasons.

The tale of Scyld Scefing tells the story of how a hero of unknown origin arrived via boat as an infant (very much like the story of Moses). He later became a well-loved and heroic king, particularly associated with peace. This story is alluded to in the Rune poem for Inguz, as well as in *Beowulf*. Scyld was the mythic progenitor of one of the Danish royal lines, the Scyldings. Some scholars, like Ellis-Davidson and Branston, see a parallel between the story of Scyld Scefing and that of Frey, pointing out that Frey often travels by means of a magic ship named Skiðblaðnir and is also strongly associated with peace.

Despite much of the ambiguity about his origins, thankfully we do know something of how his cultic practices were enacted. It seems that the Vanir like processions. Part of what has come down to us in the surviving sources indicates that Frey's image, accompanied by priests or priestesses was carried in a cart from town to town. I know of several contemporary Heathens who, at the holidays, take their sacred statues and images in their cars for processionals around their town. One woman did this regularly with a Njord statue, taking him to the beach, asperging him with sea water, and returning home. He would ride on the dashboard and she would play Nordic music on the car CD player. She felt that he liked this immensely.

In addition to regular processionals, Simek notes that it was not uncommon for a boar to be sacrificed to Frey at Yule, to ensure good harvest and peace in the coming year. This boar was considered very sacred and was known as the *sonargoltr*.(Simek, p. 270-272, 298). While animal *blót*, or sacrificial ritual, is only slowly starting to become regularly practiced again in contemporary Heathenry, many modern Heathens honor Frey in early spring with a ritual to bless the fields (or any fruitful, creative endeavor) called "The Charming of the Plow." He is also often honored at Lammas, or Frey-faxi, on July 31. This is a harvest holiday and marks the end of the gathering season. It is here that some modern devotees of Frey believe that he is cut down and sacrificed for the fecundity of the land, only to be reborn with the coming year.

I am not dedicated to Frey in any way, but I respect him immensely. Certainly I have received many blessings from his hands. I maintain a very small altar to the Vanir in my home and I make offerings, usually of wine and flowers, regularly. My own impression of Frey is that he takes after his mother in his connection to the land and his love of rich soil and growing things (whereas I've always felt Freya takes after her father, with a love of the sea). I know that several god-poles, wooden poles with the image of a Deity carved on them, have been raised honoring Frey and many Heathens that I know have shrines to him in their homes. I have found that his presence is a joyful one, a golden, shining light that cannot be denied and that drives out all spiritual ichor.

I know that the concept of deity-possession is quite controversial in modern Heathenry, but I have witnessed two rituals wherein Frey possessed a priest. Ironically the one fragment of lore that could be taken to support possessory practice within the ancient religions (but is usually categorically interpreted differently), involves Frey. In the *Ynglinga Saga*, we hear of a man who impersonated Frey. He was carried in a cart from village to village and was honored as if he were the God incarnate. The priestess accompanying him was later impregnated by him and this was seen as a great good omen ... at least until he was unmasked as an imposter. Those in modern Heathenry who believe that there is a historical precedent for divine possession within the religion will point to this passage and note that no one seemed surprised that a man might be embodying Frey. No one contested this possibility, nor the possibility that the priestess could be impregnated by a man who was Frey. This points to the fact, by this reasoning, that the idea of the Gods possessing the bodies of humans was not unknown. Others, however, interpret the passage differently and ignore that particular set of theological implications altogether.

Many modern *Seidhr* or *spae* workers feel that there is a connection between Frey and male practitioners of these arts. It seems that many Heathen gay men feel a connection to this God who accepts love and sexuality in all its myriad forms happily. Certainly with any esoteric practices like spae-craft, men who engaged in these practices were historically considered at best gender-deviant and at worst "ergi" or completely unmanly. There is one reference in Saxo Grammaticus to cross-dressing priests of Frey, who behaved in an effeminate manner, dancing about with clothing adorned with bells (Gundarsson, Our Troth, 189). I have heard several discussions within contemporary Heathenry to the possibility of Morris dancing having had its origins in old rites of Frey, specifically because of the reference to bells and dancing about in Saxo. It might be interesting to see this taken a step further within contemporary Northern Tradition sects to Frey being invoked by those in the performing arts. So far, this has not, however, occurred. The possibility points to the ways in which traditional practices can be adapted for the modern world, a tension which deeply informs contemporary Reconstructionist Paganisms and with which they must, in an ongoing way, contend.

In closing, it seems that with his associations not only with abundance and sexuality but even moreso with peace and peace-making, that Frey's wisdom is needed in the modern community now more than ever. This is a god that uprooted himself from his homeland and dwelt amongst those who had one time had been his enemies to maintain peace between nations. This is a god who knows how to make healthy compromise, and moreover how to bring fruitfulness to those compromises. Given the vitriolic nature of the ideological currents and debates so prevalent within the Northern Tradition today (even over whether Northern Tradition is an acceptable umbrella term!) I can think of no better Deity to invoke and make offerings to than the one who knows all about the sometimes terrible price of peace.

Bibliography

Branston, Brian. *The Lost Gods of England.* New York: Oxford University Press, 1974.

Ellis Davidson, Hilda. *Gods and Myths of the Viking Age.* New York: Barnes & Noble Books, 1996.

Gundarsson, Kveldulf, ed. *Our Troth.* Booksurge Publishing 2007.

-----. *Teutonic Religion: Folk Beliefs & Practices of the Northern Tradition.* St. Paul: Llewellyn Press, 1993.

Krasskova, Galina. *Exploring the Northern Tradition.* Franklin Lakes, NJ: New Page Books, 2005.

Sheffield, Ann Gróa. *Frey, God of the World.* Lulu.com, 2007.

Simek, Rudolf. *Dictionary of Northern Mythology.* Cambridge, UK: D.S. Brewer, 1993.

Tacitus. *On Britain and Germany.* Trans. H. Mattingly. Harmondsworth, Middlesex: Penguin Books, 1948.

Turville-Petre, E. O. G. *Myth and Religion of the North: The Religion of Ancient Scandinavia.* New York: Holt, Rinehart and Winston, Inc., 1964.

The Golden One
Raven Kaldera

> *Corn and grain*
> > *Rain and sun*
> *Sun must fall*
> > *All to grow*
> *Open hand*
> > *And to feed*
> *Seed to corn*
> > *Horn and need*
> *To seed.*

–*from* **Golden One,**
the song we wrote for Frey (see pg 115)

I first met Frey while journeying in Vanaheim.

I should clarify that statement a bit. As a Northern-Tradition shaman, one of the things that I do is to travel astrally through the Nine Worlds, running errands for humans and wights alike. I happened to be traveling through Vanaheim during the third of the year (Vanaheim time) that Frey dwells there—the autumn to winter period. I let it be known that I wanted to meet him, and he graciously assented to come to me there.

I'd met many, many Gods face to face, but I'd never had the reaction to any of them that I had to him. He was tall and golden and beautiful and turned me completely into a stammering, adoring schoolkid. It was more than just the respect and reverence one is moved to feel when in the presence of divine Power; this was pie-eyed adoration, the kind of thing that makes teenagers camp outside hotels for mere glimpses of rock-star idols. All I could think about was how beautiful he was, how I wanted to bask in his aura ... and then, after that had gone on for all of two minutes, how stupidly sexually attracted I was to him.

It must be understood that I'm the last person to be prone to such things. I'm a Hel's man; I've served dark gods and done their often painful work for decades. I'm old, cynical, and pessimistic, and the internal darkness that is wound through me and that makes me appropriate for this Work, generally makes me impervious to things of the Light. Yet when Frey cast his gaze on me, I was dazzled. He was gentle and good-humored about it, and asked nothing more of me than I was willing, even eager, to offer up to him. That's the way his relationship has been with me ever since—I give out of love, and he asks nothing more than that.

> *Would you bring light to the dark?*
> *Would you sing the summer's song?*
> *Would you speed the growing,*
> *Rushing toward the coming pain?*

In Dale Cannon's book *Six Ways of Being Religious* (Wadsworth Publishing Company, 1996), a tome that is dry as toast but filled with wonderful theological concepts, he discusses six paths or worship that are found within each religion, some more so than others. (I highly recommend this book to Pagans who want to think deeply about the theology of their faith, even though it has only Christian and Buddhist examples; it's inspiringly easy to extrapolate Pagan examples anyway.) Some of these paths, like the Way of Sacred Rite, the Way of Mystical Quest, and the Way of Right Action, I practice as part of a group religious tradition, for the people I serve. The Way of Reasoned Inquiry taught me to appreciate religious scholarship among the reconstructionists as a valid form of worship, even when I find them frustratingly limited and fearful in their scope. The Way of Shamanic Mediation is my life, my toolkit, dedicated entirely to Hela who owns me and uses me for the betterment of the world.

The sixth path, though, the Way of Devotion, eluded me until I met Frey. The Way of Devotion is about having what born-again Christians call "a personal relationship with Jesus"; it is characterized by, as Cannon says, "wholehearted adoration, devotional surrender to (its) transforming grace, and trust in (its) providential care". As a shaman, dealing with Gods and wights is almost ordinary for me. I respect and revere them, but for me the kind of divine contact that would seem inspirational to most people is simply something that gets me out of bed at 3 a.m.—*again*—to do some obscure job. My view of religion would seem frighteningly pragmatic to most folk. Frey gave me back my sense of devotion. I don't work for him, and so I am free to love him with no strings attached. That's an amazing gift for a cynical old spirit-worker.

I did ask him for a favor, once, and he did request payment, but that's only fair. It was a big ongoing favor. He requested that I put a Frey pole up in my back field, and that I would allow him to use my body as a public horse one day a year. I agreed willingly, even though deity-possession was something of an ambivalent activity for me. I'd been introduced to it very much against my will (a common theme for nearly everything in my shamanic training) and it often felt like a violation. My boss, Hela, let me know that I was going to have to get a better attitude about it—what rock star wants a surly, cantankerous limo driver? There seemed no better way to start opening myself up with a better attitude than to offer my flesh to Frey; my relationship with him was clean enough that I could trust him and not feel violated.

On Lammas of that year we put the pole up in my back field. My wife carved it of cherry wood—one of Frey's trees—primitive, but with a smile and a huge phallus. We threw sacrifices into the hole and stood him up while our Pagan choir sang the song that he'd dictated to me. Then, the next night, I deliberately asked to be ridden for the first time in two decades of being forced to it. He came in like a shaft of golden light, warming and healing, and off he went to talk with (and tumble with) my partner, who was making his own physical offering, and came out of the experience with a big grin on his face. It was the least emotionally complicated time I'd ever had as a horse, and it went a long way towards attitude adjustment.

Since then, I've been ridden by Frey as part of our big Lammas ritual for the last two years. I don't drink alcohol, but on that day I drink blessed home-brewed beer as part of the work of bringing Him into me. I am dressed in His vestments—yellow linen tunic embroidered with gold wheat sheaves, crown of grain, specially gifted golden torc, and His sacred phallus—and then I'm in the back seat, or more likely unconscious in the trunk, and He holds court among my people. Afterwards, I listen to their tales. We noticed that Frey will pick out certain specific people and blow gently onto their foreheads or heart chakras, "blowing light into them", as He says, "a light in darkness." These people are usually the sort whose spiritual job is to be light-bringers themselves in some way, but who are often troubled by depression or woes that get in the way of it. They report that Frey's breath creates a tiny spark of permanent light in them that can be blown on and grown, no matter how hard times get. After I wrote about that on my website and in my book, I was contacted by other people who had met with Frey and had this same experience—and were amazed that they'd found their personal gnosis verified by strangers several states away.

> *Would you do what must be done?*
> *Would you hold back nothing, not*
> *Your breath, not your body,*
> *Not your fear, not your pride?*

Two similar complaints that I've heard repeatedly out of Pagans is that all the deities of love are female, and so are the deities of marriage. In the Norse pantheon, Frey is an exception to both of those generalities—but then, hey, we have a female Sunna and a male Mani, right? While Freya does hold the sort of "hat" that Aphrodite wears for the Greek pantheon—love goddess, sacred whore, and golden maiden—and Frigga is the primary deity of marriage, Frey is happy to be invoked for both. There's a lot of emphasis on the "fertility" aspect of his nature (due probably to a mix of people reading too much anthropology and an obsession with his huge cock), but he is more than just a god of Sex. He is also a god of Love, whatever form that may take. For Frey, yes, Love is very sexual, very physical, but he can also make love with a smile, a touch, a direct gaze.

I once went to a wonderfully inspired ritual to Freya where the officiating Freyaswoman running it called upon her in a circle with four doors, each corresponding to her four aspects. I'd never heard it put so cleanly and perfectly before: the golden love goddess, the green spring fertility maiden, the warrior in scarlet and white, and the seidhkona wrapped in dark mists. I could also see equal correspondences in her twin brother ... with one exception. In giving up his sword to Gerda's family as a bride-price, Frey lost any role as Warrior. He gave that away out of Love, and I can think of no more wonderful defining characteristic of a male god of Love. Like Freya, he is fertility—although where she rules the Spring, he is the Autumn harvest. Like her, he teaches about Love, although his teachings go in two different directions.

His connection to his sister is both ritual and erotic, which makes not a few people uncomfortable. As the sacred fertility pair of the Vanir, they are required to have an erotic relationship so that the crops will grow, the flocks and herds increase, the flowers spring up and the fruits ripen. It's part of the magic. As part of his connection with Freya, he embodies the same kind of transpersonal Aphroditic-style love that she does, where everyone you lie with, even if only for an hour, is beautiful in their own way, but no more so than anyone else. He opens his arms and his gaze to men, women, and everyone else, because for him it isn't who you do it with, it's how you do it. An Odin's man once commented on Odin's bisexuality by saying that for the Old Man, it isn't about sexual preference so much as it's about sexual power. Is there power in this sexual act? Well, we'll be doing it, then! Similarly, for Frey and Freya it's about sexual joy. Does this sex act reverberate with the clouds, the trees, the earth beneath your feet? Does it inspire gratitude for the gift of your own flesh? Then, really, the combination of bodies involved is irrelevant.

However, unlike his sister, Frey is also a god of marriage—committed, intensely personal love, bound to land and stone and rings of metal, focused wholly on one person. Frey is completely capable of maintaining both of these states perfectly, simultaneously focusing on a spouse in a personal relationship and spreading his golden joy transpersonally to all who throw themselves at him, and thus is an inspiration for both monogamous and polyamorous people everywhere.

Of course, one can't speak of Frey as a god of marriage without bringing up his giantess-wife Gerda. She came into my life soon after he did, quietly and without fanfare, which is how she lives her very principled life. Gerda is the opposite of Frey in so many ways—dark where he is light, reserved where he is outgoing, modest where he is flamboyant, private where he is public, self-enclosed where he gives freely—and utterly, unswervingly solid where he may be prone to wavering with his feelings. He surprised us when, the first year that I horsed him publicly, he requested beforehand that a horse be made available for her as well. A female spirit-worker who owed Frey a favor volunteered, and she arrived. We had never had a divine couple present together before, and we were quickly reminded of why Frey and Gerda are invoked at weddings, why their figures were stamped on bits of gilt for happiness and contentment. The two of them act like newlyweds when together, no matter how long they have been married—eating honey off of each others' fingers, openly affectionate, with loving gazes at each other.

Ours may be the only group where Frey and Gerda come together. Other groups who utilize god-possession to bring down the Northern gods report that Frey is only coupled with Freya at their gatherings, and Gerda does not come. Gerda, apparently, will only show herself in a place where no one present is likely to denigrate her race, which means that she will shun most Ásatrú/Heathen groups. Our group, being Neo-Pagan, doesn't care about such politics, and so we are able to give the two of them the gift of being together at such a gathering, if only for a little while.

The marriage of Frey and Gerda was met with consternation by nearly all the families, clans, allies, and kinship groups involved. This means that while Frigga and her husband Odin are the sacred couple called upon for marriages that are acceptable to the greater society, Frey and Gerda are called upon to bless unions that are not. They are happy to bless queer or polyamorous weddings, and any "mixed marriage"—a union where two people come from drastically different cultures/religions/worldviews and constant, patient compromise must be invoked regularly in order to keep the marriage surviving. This is their territory, their specialty.

Gerda, in her quiet and uncompromising way, refuses to live among those who hate her kin, and refuses to bear children to her husband's hostage-oaths; thus the God of fertility has a barren marriage. For this reason and for many others, Frey and Gerda out of all the Gods and wights have the most to lose from Ragnarok, and the most to gain from widespread peace between all peoples. This combination of events has crystallized to make Frey into the God of Frith, the Peacemaker between peoples, the Unweaponed God who values Love over War every time. Infighting between groups dismays him, and he will push for peace even at the risk of seeming "unmanly", which gives him a lesser reputation among some overly-macho Ásatrú folk. What most Aesir-followers don't know is that Gerda is just as much a goddess of frithmaking as her husband, only she plies her end of that thread on the opposite side, among her people, her Gods, and the humans who work with them.

To work tirelessly for peace in the face of war, understanding in the face of argument, compassion in the face of fear; to stand open-handed while facing a sword of hurt and anger; to swallow one's pride and do what is effective to foster communication rather than what makes one feel righteous; these are not cowardly acts. They require supreme amounts of courage and self-sacrifice, and only the very brave ever manage to adhere to them full-time, without giving in to self-indulgent defensiveness. Frey and Gerda's road is a hard one. It is much easier to join the roaring communal war-band with their unchallenged bigotries and assumptions. Being a peacemaker can get you killed. Ask any diplomat in a war zone.

Would you give your life for love?
Would you die to feed them all?
Would you go a-willing like the man to his bride?

Frey's best-known role is that of God of Sacrifice, the one who willingly gives his life that others may live. Here, as God of Fertility, he wears the crown of Ing, the Corn King, John Barleycorn. I connect with Frey the Fertility-God in a very different way than I connect with Frey the Love God who was invoked at my wedding ceremony. Here, the connection is so familiar as to be casual, or practically unnoticed, because the "dailyness" of my life as a farmer and homesteader sometimes gets in the way of more obvious ritual.

I live on a small homestead with my wife—who is descended from Frey, with a maternal maiden name of Ingerson, and who brews her own beer—and with my boyfriend. Most people think that our lives are full of exciting sexual interludes, but the truth is that if we ever get the time, we're lucky. Most of our days are filled with milking the goats, slopping the sheep, feeding the chickens, gathering eggs, bringing in wood from the forest to light our wood cookstove, and dealing with the garden in whatever state it may be in at the moment. In a way, writing the book *EarthBound: Pagan*

Homesteading was also an offering to Frey, although I dedicated it to many God/desses. Living in the way that we do is more than just a nod to sustainability, or a way to get cheap organic food, or a fun hobby; it's an act of worship. I understand the cycle of John Barleycorn deeply, because I have ripped up rows of bravely waving carrots, hacked down fields of corn, and butchered out livestock to feed myself and my family. Life feeds on life. Something must die that we all can live. Everything I put in my mouth is sacred, and I need to remember that.

I am, among other things, a plant shaman. I talk to plants. I've had amazing conversations with Grandmother and Grandfather plant spirits. I've spoken with trees. Part of why I am not a vegetarian (besides the fact that I like meat) is that to be a vegetarian for reasons of animal-killing-is-cruel is to privilege animals over plants. I realize that this is a view that is going to be difficult for most people even to begin to understand, but it is something that I have learned from Frey (and, to an extent, from Herne the ancient Hunter). To say that it's not OK to kill a chicken, but it is OK to rip up a fresh carrot and eat it, that's saying that the chicken has value and the carrot doesn't, that the carrot's life is irrelevant, that its death can be ignored. It is, after all, more alien to us than the chicken. Acceptable death, in this worldview, is based on xenophobia—the more like me it is, the less acceptable it is to kill it. Plants don't talk or move around, therefore they aren't *really* alive.

Yet the myth of John Barleycorn says something completely different. People wept and mourned the grain that was cut down just as thoroughly as the calf that went to the slaughter, because they understood that *all* life was worthy of revering. The grain—the very symbol of the life that was sacrificed—is a plant, not an animal. I *can* talk to plants, and I would far rather kill a chicken than cut down a grandfather tree. (I've tried to talk to chickens. Grandfather trees are more intelligent conversationalists.) More to the point, both are equal manifestations of the Sacrificed God, as are the cow and the carrot. Pretending that one sort of life is more alive than another sort is a blasphemous form of denial. We cannot use such denial to wash the blood off of our hands ... because when it is seen through respectful eyes, that blood is sacred, regardless of species.

I know that Frey does not like modern agribusiness practices at all. I know that they pain him, that he is saddened by the way that we (mis)treat our food. He is a God of Food, something we like to forget. Really, when it comes down to it, that's the first reason for fertility. Food. We will still need it even at negative population growth. What people need to understand, though, is that for Frey, there is no difference between a chicken bred to have a breast so large that it can barely stand and to grow so fast that it must be caged in a foot-square box or it will break its spindly legs, living a short life deprived of sun and dirt, debeaked and crowded and fed with hormones and antibiotics ... and a soybean plant that is genetically engineered to survive being soaked in round after round of deadly poison, growing in sterile dirt fed only with chemicals in a huge monocropped field, processed into oblivion and heated until it develops trans fatty acids, and packed into a soy-paste product designed to make someone feel good about not eating that chicken.

There is no difference, to Frey. No difference. It is all food. It is all life. It is all disrespect.

If I sound angry and militant here, I apologize. This issue does not make Frey angry. It makes him sad. And anything that makes him sad ... makes me angry. I am still very much a Jotun-blooded creature of darkness. Like his beloved.

> *Would you do what must be done?*
> *Would you be the Golden One?*
> *Would you spring up laughing,*
> *Trusting fate like the grain?*

Sacrifice. This brings us around again to the last path that he shares with Freya, although again she is more well-known for that. She is the greatest of Seidhkonas, the witch who teaches the magic that (supposedly) makes women powerful and men unmanly. Frey understands this magic too—how could he not, being her twin?—

but is less known for it. Frey's path in this is where sacrifice meets sex, where we remember that the Ing-man who faced the priestess with the sickle was castrated and flung into the swamp to die. They say that if he lived, he was allowed to live on as a woman, but a magical one.

One thing that I grow more sure of all the time is that there are at least two cults of Freysmen, or were, and will be again. One is the farmer, the husbandman, the husband and father who lays his seed into his beloved to make children, into the earth to bring it fertility. He sacrifices with his labor, and with his commitment to frith. The other is the *ergi* priests with their skirts hung with tinkling bells, their cross-gender high-pitched songs, who gave up that most Freylike of qualities—physical manhood—in order to learn the Mysteries and the Deep Magics.

Tribal shamans in any tradition will all tell you: The Spirit in charge of any sacred thing can both give it and take it away. You pray to the smallpox god to protect you from infectious diseases. You pray to the lightning-thrower to spare your thatch roof in the storm. You ask the God of Sacrifice with his huge erection to give you shamanic powers, and he responds: Will you sacrifice this, for the Mysteries? Will you become something between male and female, forever, where everyone can see, in exchange for that power?

This is the path of Frey that starts with the sickle cut, the scythe swing, the moment of blood and pain. This is the Frey who walks the Hel Road, who goes to the very Gates of Death and back, who hosts the miracle of rebirth. The difference between these two cults have nothing to do with being gay or straight, with who you want to bang bits with. That, as we've already determined, is irrelevant to Frey. The difference between these two cults is about being *ergi*, being publicly cross-gender, mixed-gender, outsider, mediator, Walker Between Worlds, catalyst of discomfort, infertile vessel of shamanic power, and ... not.

As someone who is transsexual, whose fertility was long ago offered up as a sacrifice, I know this road. I wear the skirts and the jingling bells, in honor of those *ergi* folk who lived before me and left signs on this dark path. These are my ancestors, even though they left no children. Frey is the Light That Descends To The Darkness And Arises Again, just as his sister is the Light That Seeks Upwards And Descends Again. If he didn't love and understand the darkness, he couldn't love Gerda. He couldn't love the blade that takes his manhood and his life, every year. He couldn't love all the many races of the Nine Worlds to whom he holds out his hands in frith, each with their various fears and wraths and pettinesses and obstinacies.

He couldn't love me.

Hail to the Light that descends to the Dark,
That lights it with Love,
That never fails to bring tears of joy
To old, old eyes.
Corn and grain,
Open hand,
Seed to corn to seed.

Oimelc Rite for Frey: Ocean's Son

Raven Kaldera

This is a solitary rite honoring Frey as the son of Njord. It is especially for adults who have rifts between themselves and their parents, and would call on Frey and Njord to help heal the wounds so that a better relationship can be forged. It was inspired by Seawalker's Bremen recipe honoring Frey as Njord's son. For this rite, you will need a handful of grain and a bowl of cold water with sea salt dissolved in it. First, find a quiet place and sit calmly for a time. Do not think about any anguish or problems you have had with your parent-child relationship. Concentrate on how good it would be if all was well between you. Then take the handful of grain in your hand and say:

> Ingvi-Frey, Son of Vanaheim, I call out to you.
> You knew love from the very beginning,
> Golden child of earth goddess
> And doting sea god, ever proud
> Of your heart and your worth.
> Yet my mortal life was not as blessed,
> There is a great gulf between myself
> And those who bore me into this world.
> I cannot fill the chasm of darkness
> That looms between us. I cannot find the way.
> I call on you, Ingvi-Frey, Good Son,
> Help me to step beyond my own darkness
> And find forgiveness, and love,
> And even appreciation of their hearts.
> Bless this fragile bond between us
> And help me find the way, if it can be found.

Dip your hand in the salt water and make a mark over your heart, and say:

Wise Njord, Father of Vanaheim, I call out to you.
You gave love from the very beginning.
Your children are your wealth, your hopes,
Your greatest treasures, and you saw nothing
But beauty and worthiness in their eyes.
Yet my mortal childhood was not as blessed.
There is great strife between myself
And those who bore me into this world.
I cannot stop the looming storm
That crashes down between us, over and over.
I call on you, Goodfather Njord,
Help them to step beyond their own darknesses
And find forgiveness, and love,
And even appreciation of my heart.
Bless this fragile bond between us
And help them find the way, if it can be found.

Sprinkle the grain over the salt water, and sit waiting while it slowly absorbs water and sinks. Then pour the bowl out onto the earth, saying:

Njord's son rides in Skidbladnir, and comes to see him,
And he is proud and happy, and only joy fills his eyes,
And Ingvi embraces his father with great hopes,
Knowing that anything he says will be listened to
And seen only through eyes of love, not fear.
Skidbladnir sails into Noatun's harbor,
And Ingvi knows that it will always be home.
Hail Frey, Son of Vanaheim.
Hail Njord, Father of Vanaheim.
May your blessings fall upon us in every way.

Wait three days, and then attempt contact. Remember, as you go into this hard work, that Frey would have you suspend judging and reactive fears until the contact plays fully out.

Oimelc Recipes for a Frey Feast

Pork Hocks in Beer (Schweinshaxen)
Seawalker

Ingredients:
2 meaty pork hocks
1 leek
1 celery stalk
1 onion
Salt
Black peppercorns
2 tbsp. butter
Enough flour to make gravy
Pinch of cumin
A good craft beer

Preheat oven to 350 degrees. Dice the vegetables. Put the pork hocks, vegetables, salt, and pepper in a pot and cover with beer; cover and cook 2 to 3 hours or until meat is tender. Do not overcook. Remove meat and get the oven up to 425 degrees. Melt the butter in a pan and lay in the meat with a small amount of the cooking liquid. Sprinkle meat with cumin. Bake 30 minutes, moistening about every 5 minutes with more of the cooking liquid. When browned, lift out the meat and pour the drippings into the cooking liquid. Heat cooking liquid and add enough flour to make gravy. Serve the pork hocks with the gravy separate for pouring.

Farmer Cheese Dumplings
Seawalker

Ingredients:
½ cup dried currants, soaked in water or apple cider until plump
1 pound farmer cheese (or cottage cheese that has been sieved,
          mashed and drained)
2 tbsp. sugar
Pinch of salt
2 eggs
2 tbsp. flour
2 tbsp. cornstarch
Half a loaf of stale bread, soaked in milk

Combine the cheese, sugar, salt, and eggs, and then stir in the flour and cornstarch. If the mix is still very wet, add a little more flour. Drain the currants and bread and mix them in with your hands. Again, add flour if the mix is too wet. With wet hands, form the dough into dumplings and cook for ten minutes in water that is already simmering pretty well, but not quite boiling. Drain and serve with powdered sugar sprinkled on top.

Kale-Month Wurst
Raven Kaldera

The Anglo-Saxons called February Kale-Monath or Kale Month (as well as Solmonath) because Kale was what they had left to eat. This dish is especially good to celebrate Frey's relationship as Njord's son. For hundreds of years, the city dignitaries of Bremen were invited to dine on shipboard every February by the captains of the fleet's ships before they sailed out of Bremerhaven. They were served a dish of kale and sausages very like this one; the sausages were traditionally *pinkelwurst*.

Ingredients:
3 pounds curly kale, finely chopped
1/3 cup bacon fat (save it from bacon frying)
1 diced onion
½ pound diced bacon
1 tbsp. rolled oats
1 pound wurst, or German sausage, of your choice
Salt
Water

Blanch the kale briefly in boiling water and drain. In a saucepan, melt the bacon fat and sauté the onion. Add the kale, salt, bacon, and sausage. Cover and cook over low heat for an hour. Keep checking on it—when the kale is tender, stir in the oats and cook a little longer.

Frith-Maker

Prayer for the Frith-Maker
Ari

Hail Frey, Frith-Maker of the Gods
Who works against the warlike odds.
You ride to war when it is needed,
But innocent cries are always heeded
And far rather would you speak for peace
And sue that words should make war cease.
Hostage for your people's cause,
You remember how it was,
And yet you hold out hands to gather
Each and every heart together.
Your very wedding day a call
For truce and understanding all,
Your very flesh reined to this path,
With hands and kiss you strive and laugh,
You do this work each night in bed,
Each day in sun, each word that's said.
You are a voice of calm and reason,
Hail to Frey, Lord of Good Seasons!

Prayer for Light

Joshua Tenpenny

Hail Frey, my Fulltrui, god of my heart,
You are with me now,
as you always have been,
and always will be,
in times of need, and of plenty,
in times of folly, and of wisdom,
in times of sorrow, and of joy.

Help me to remember
that the spark of your light
which resides in my heart
can be kindled into a bright flame,
of love, and of hope, and of joy,
if only I will it,
no matter how bleak the circumstances.

Help me to remember
that Love is an infinite resource,
an inexhaustible supply,
which does not need to be saved
for some special occasion,
or measured out by the teaspoonful,
given only when earned.

Help me to remember,
that I can share this light with others,
without passing judgment on them,
and that withholding it harms me
far more than it harms them.

Help me find the strength
to release anger, fear, and despair,
and choose joy.
In your name, may I always choose joy.

Prayer Beads for Frey
Raven Kaldera

There are a number of variations for Frey prayer beads floating around, but this is the small set that I made to carry around. Like this book, it runs through the seasons, but unlike this book, it starts with Yule. This set is truly mixed media—stone, glass, ceramic, wood, nuts. The names of the runes can be sung or chanted. Some are Norse and some are Anglo-Saxon—I just use the names that come easily to my tongue, whichever those happen to be.

(Large Nut)
Hail Ingvi Frey, Golden One whose love grows tall every summer, is cut down every autumn, and grows again in the spring. May peace and good seasons walk with me on my road.

(Golden Pearl Glass Bead)
Hail to the Gift-Giver! May I always be grateful for what I have been given.

(Light Rose Quartz Bead)
Gyfu Gyfu Gyfu Gyfu

(Amber Bead)
Sacrifice, usefulness, and joy.

(Moss Agate Bead)
Hail to the Son of Vanaheim! May I always respect those who came before me.

(Blue Ceramic Bead)
Laguz Laguz Laguz Laguz

(Amber Bead)
Sacrifice, usefulness, and joy.

(Clear Glass Bead)
Hail to the Frith-Maker! May I be a force of peace in the world.

(Pale Orange Carnelian Bead)
Mannaz Mannaz Mannaz Mannaz

(Amber Bead)
Sacrifice, usefulness, and joy.

(Cherry Quartz Bead)
Hail to the God of Love! May my flesh always be a source of pleasure and joy.

(Aventurine Bead)
Feoh Feoh Feoh Feoh

(Amber Bead)
Sacrifice, usefulness, and joy.

(Large Nut)
Hail Ingvi Frey, Golden One whose love grows tall every summer, is cut down every autumn, and grows again in the spring. May peace and good seasons walk with me on my road.

(Golden Cat's Eye Glass Bead)
Hail to the Light-Bringer! May the spark of hope inside me always burn.

(Yellow Jade Bead)
Wunjo Wunjo Wyn Wyn

(Amber Bead)
Sacrifice, usefulness, and joy.

(Amber Glass Faceted Bead)
Hail to the Golden One! May I never forget the sacrifice of all that dies that I might live.

(Blood-Red Glass Bead)
Ing Ing Ing Ing

(Amber Bead)
Sacrifice, usefulness, and joy.

(Brown Glass Bead with Gold Lampwork Wreath)
Hail to the Marriage-God! May all my relationships be true and faithful.

(Green Ceramic Bead)
Chalc Chalc Chalc Chalc

(Amber Bead)
Sacrifice, usefulness, and joy.

(Wooden Bead)
Hail to the Harvest King! May I sow the future and reap joy.

(Unakite Bead)
Jera Jera Jera Jera

(Amber bead)
Sacrifice, usefulness, and joy.

(Large Nut)
Hail Ingvi Frey, Golden One whose love grows tall every summer, is cut down every autumn, and grows again in the spring. May peace and good seasons walk with me on my road.

He Who Looses Fetters
Svartesol

> *Frey is best*
> *of all the exalted gods*
> *in the Æsir's courts:*
> *no maid he makes to weep,*
> *no wife of man,*
> *and from bonds looses all.*
> –Lokasenna

I swore oaths to Frey in February of 2004. At the time I identified as Asatru, and thought that was what I was "supposed" to be doing with myself spiritually. After I dedicated to Frey, His family moved to the forefront. I had already had a difficult time connecting with the Aesir, but for the sake of "doing it right" I continued to try reaching out to Them. By 2006 it was clear this approach wasn't working, and I stumbled upon the word "Vanatru" for the first time. I thought this was a rather accurate descriptor, but when I applied it to myself, some of my Heathen friends protested. A year later, I began to have serious doubts about remaining within Heathenry.

As my sense of belonging with the Vanir deepened, I started seeing a distinct difference between Their preferred forms of worship and business as usual in Heathenry. I was still convinced this was where Frey wanted me, and so I tried to change things. This did not go so well.

What I didn't realize until too late is that my futile attempts at remaining within "the Heathen community" had less to do with my desire to serve Frey, and more to do with my own pride and longstanding issues. A recurring theme in my life is being bullied. I had left schools and jobs due to my experience with being on the receiving end of bullying. Cycles will repeat themselves until they are broken. I did not want to leave an entire religion behind for parts unknown, because to my way of thinking, at that time, it would be "letting them win". Unfortunately, continuing to "fight the good fight" meant I was losing.

In my fifth year of walking with Frey, I gained a leadership position within a Heathen organization. I thought I had "won", but it turned out that made me a bigger target for criticism. Due to pressure from some of the circles I traveled in, I wound up publicly hurting people I cared about because they had unpopular opinions and practices. This left a bad feeling in my conscience. Also, I often had to stifle what I really wanted to say, especially regarding mystical experiences, to "fit in". The task of fitting in became unbearably uncomfortable, and after several months in this position I resigned. Not only did I resign from the organization, but I took a hiatus from doing any religious activities.

Frey's mother, Nerthus, showed up at that point and gave me a lifeline. While my devotional and ritual life was still on hold, I was asked to dedicate each month to a different God in the Vanir pantheon (known or suspected to be Vanic) and learn from Them. I was initially confused by some of the experiences I had, especially with regards to instructions given, but realized after a few months it was to prepare me for the road less traveled—where I had been headed all along, but dragged my feet.

During this time I began to consider the possibility of returning to Wicca, where I had started out. I felt it was necessary to get back to my roots and rediscover why I had become Pagan, and what was important to me. I had gotten so caught up in "doing it right" that I lost connection and purpose. I loved Frey enough that I was willing to be seen by others as a traitor, or a coward, or an otherwise dishonorable person for converting, so long as I could continue to worship Him. But also, Wicca is extremely compatible with the Vanir. (I have known of Witches who worship the Aesir, especially Odin who has connections with magic, but I think it fits Vanir worship better.) The names Frey and Freya literally mean 'Lord' and 'Lady'. The Great Rite, whether performed literally or symbolically between the priest and priestess, is a beautiful expression of the celebration of sex and the fertility that Frey and Freya give to the worlds. Many of the Wiccan Sabbats are based in English folk customs that ultimately seem to have their origins in Vanic customs (e.g. the Maypole). Nothing seems more Vanic than honoring the elements and the directions of the Land. The pentacle can be seen as representing the Vanic lore of Star Mother (the star) mating with Herne (the circle) and making the world(s).

It was up to Frey what He wanted, but I was willing to truly listen to what He had to say, without my preconceived notions.

To my surprise, He thoroughly encouraged it. On Imbolc 2010, I re-dedicated myself to Wicca, before Frey and Nerthus. I had a beautiful Imbolc ritual with my partner, who supported my return to the Craft. I immediately felt a sense of relief—a wave of freedom washing over me, and cleansing away the toxicity built up for years. I had, finally, won, and what I won was my freedom.

However, the freedom also gave me the freedom to experience the anger and resentment I had been feeling for years, at the state of Heathenry. It also presented me with the need to take responsibility for my own motivations and actions. I had to decide where to go from here.

Even though I am considered someone at the forefront of the Vanatru movement, I prefer that Vanatru not have a central authority. I am but one person on one path. Your mileage will vary. Some of us are Wiccan, some of us are Heathen, some of us are Druids. The important thing is that each of us worships the Gods in the way They want us to, and thus has our spiritual needs met. What Frey requires from me is not necessarily what He wants from someone else.

And what Frey requires of me is freedom. I do not believe the Gods are omnibenevolent and want sunshine and rainbows for all of us. However, I am a melancholy person by nature. It is easier for me to be depressed and angry than it is to experience joy and celebration. For years, I focused on the sacrificial aspect of Frey, who is cut down to feed the fields in exchange for the harvest—a gift for a gift. I got caught up in His sorrow for the world, and how His sacrifice becomes more and more poignant each year. What I continually need to remember is that He does return, to keep the promise of the cycles of life-death-rebirth, and to fill us with vitality and renewal. If I am to bear His light within me and the hope He brings, I cannot do so if I am all bound up.

Frey has given me many gifts over the years—a partner, a home, friendships, and health. Yet the greatest gift Frey has given me is freedom—the ability to approach Him freely, based on what He would like from me, not what I think other people think He would like from me. My experience with going back to Wicca even if others disapprove helped to bring closure with the other times in my life I had been bullied. Frey not only heals the land, He can heal our hearts.

So, it is with a glad heart, and a free spirit, that I take His wain down the road less traveled. When the moon is full, I give thanks to the Lord and Lady for Their love which is the force of life. I cast the circle and have come full circle. I wear the pentacle proudly, as a symbol of my faith, and at a deeper level, the stars that shine in the darkness—the light that Frey gave to me, that no man may put out again.

My Vanaheim Ordeal

Galina Krasskova

(This was one of a series of ordeals, one for each world. While the primary focus of this ordeal was Nerthus, the mother of Frey, He also asked a separate ordeal of me, that I might understand the ways of the Vanir. I include both stories here.)

I do not belong to the Vanir. I am owned instead by Odin, as anyone who has read my work can easily ascertain. I also have a strong affinity for Loki and Sigyn. Until recently, with the exception of Gerda, I had not had much interaction with any of the Vanir or other Deities commonly associated with Them. It was, however at Odin's behest that I first sought out Vanaheim, as part of a series of nine ritual ordeals (one for each of the nine worlds) that He bade me undergo. I began with Helheim and was slowly working my way up the Tree. It was early May when the time to visit Vanaheim came due.

Each ordeal in this extensive cycle has given me access to one of the Nine Worlds and each has been governed by one of the Deities who rule in that particular world. With each ordeal, I gained knowledge, skill and made necessary sacrifices of the self. I never knew what would be asked of me prior to the actual ordeal itself. Many of these rites have been wrenching. Nearly all have been physically painful in some way. Sandwiched as it was between my Jotunheim ordeal (which had proved emotionally quite devastating) and Alfheim (which, being a completely unknown quantity, filled me with trepidation), I had not expected Vanaheim to prove much of a challenge. It seemed pretty clear cut to me: land, dirt, cycles of land, more dirt, etc. In retrospect, my hubris amazes even me.

Thinking about it almost a year after my final ordeal in this cycle, I realize that many of us go to the Vanir with the unconscious preconception that because They are Gods of fertility, abundance, sensuality, and a thousand other things, this means that They are always gentle and kind. It doesn't matter that the sagas and sacred stories may tell us differently. No one really expects Frey, for instance, to be demanding and harsh. No one expects that an ordeal at the hands of the Vanir might be a truly difficult and painful ordeal. Bloody, painful, agonizing challenges seem more the venue of Odin and His get. I realize now that this is a most unfortunate filter of modernity peeking through and skewing the lens of devotion: Gods are Gods and sacrifice is the coin by which They often teach. Our ancestors, living a predominantly agrarian lifestyle would have recognized this well. They would have known that nature, the elements, the land itself gives no quarter. Why should the Gods to Whom those things belong?

Of course, like many Heathens, I honored the Vanir when the occasion arose as Gods of fertility, abundance, wealth, and bounty of land and sea but beyond that I gave Them little thought. I, warrior-trained, warrior-called, Valkyrie of the grimmest of Gods, had little love or respect for the secrets and mysteries these bright Gods hold. Even within my ancestral venerations, I often disparaged ancestors who were farmers, preferring instead to honor those who had served in the military, who did not make their living from the land. Furthermore, as a city dweller (a very happy city dweller) I'd had little interaction with the rhythms and cycles of the natural world, for all that I might have had abstract understanding of them. Much of this was to change with this particular ordeal.

The first part of my Vanaheim ordeal occurred late in May. A friend, colleague, shaman, and farmer agreed to facilitate for me. Nerthus was to hold the secrets for me in this particular ordeal. She was the Goddess I had to face and by whom I was to be humbled. I have heard many people describe Nerthus as a comforting, loving, gentle Mother Goddess. Mother Goddess She may indeed be but She is also terrifying, harsh, implacable and fierce. This is the Goddess referenced in Tacitus who commonly received human sacrifice as Her due, after all. She is the Mother, but not in any controlled, safe Ozzie-and-Harriet type way. She is the ultimate devouring Mother Goddess, She of the earthquake, of flood, of famine, of feasting, of the life and death of all living things, of loam and bog, silt and soil. Who better to humble this warrior's soul?

She commanded that I be buried alive. She is about life, yes, but also death and the cycles in between that connect the two. She is about the wisdom of the earth, the vicious clarity of the land that devours and from that ruthless devouring spews forth new life. A trench was dug and covered with thick netting. (Thankfully, I was not required to actually lay covered completely with dirt. I am a kinesthetic learner and needed some minor mobility to best process the lessons that were to be forthcoming.) Naked, with only prayer beads, a journal, and water to sustain me, I was committed to the pit. Of course, fittingly, I was on my menstrual cycle. It was agreed upon that once every four hours someone would come to check on me, bringing me water and a minimal amount of food (organic greens, grain, nuts) but otherwise I was permitted no human contact during this time. I was to stay until Nerthus gave me permission to depart.

Isolation is a powerful tool particularly when it is filled with the presence of a Goddess so terrifying that ancient acolytes were not permitted to gaze even upon Her unveiled images. She showed me directly the cycle of life-into-death-into-life contained in the land itself. I saw insects and spiders creeping about the leaves and dirt that filled the trench with me, creeping between roots of bushes and trees. I saw that dirt itself was not some inactive substance devoid of life (as I had always thought) but that it was the raw substance from which life is born, a living, shifting, very active biosphere. I later learned that there are more living organisms in a handful of dirt than there are human beings on the planet and so much life and death goes on there that it's not surprising Nerthus is Herself so very terrifying.

For six hours She kept me in the pit. Her lessons weren't only about the sacredness of dirt but also of the primal bond that one has with one's mother (even if not one's biological mother ... in my case, She honored my adopted mother, bringing home just how sacred and important that bond was on a wyrd level). She forced me to examine my own misogyny and distaste for the typical cultural markers of "womanhood." She is beyond any limited human conception of "female." She simply is.

Moreover, Nerthus challenged me to honor my body as I had never once honored it before. I spent years as a professional ballet dancer, a career in which neglect and harsh treatment of one's body is de rigueur. For more than half my lifetime I had looked upon my body as "the enemy". Nerthus spoke about the importance of embodiment and drove home the point that we are not separate from our bodies, but that our bodies are an integral part of how we are meant to interact with not only each other but with the Gods Themselves. This is all the more important for shamans and spirit-workers: our bodies are one of the primary interfaces through which we communicate that which comes from the Gods. Our bodies are the primary tools with which we work, the means by which we function, acquire and disseminate knowledge. Our bodies are an immense gift. The flesh and the sensorium it houses are tremendously sacred. They are the chrysalis of our souls and all the expression and growth and transformation that can lie hidden within those souls. Our bodies are important.

The ordeal took place on land which has housed a stone labyrinth for years. After six hours I was allowed to leave the pit and forced to walk around and around this sacred labyrinth, then it was back to the pit for another six hours. Eventually, I was allowed to emerge into the darkness (it was after midnight) and I made the journey, naked, barefoot, exhausted from the pit, through the woods back to my friend's house. She let me go with the understanding that I had gleaned about half of the lessons I was meant to. I knew, walking through the woods in the pitch black darkness that there would be at least one more part to my Vanaheim ordeal. I was being given leeway to process the lessons She had given me first. I had reached the point where I could comprehend nothing more from the pit.

Oddly enough, the most humbling part of the ordeal took place as She forced me to think on the bond I share with my adopted mom. I am terribly arachnophobic, so sitting in a pit with spiders and assorted insects, large spiders, was enough to nearly give me anxiety attacks. The spiders were not prepared as part of the ordeal, let me be clear about that. They were there, in their biosphere, in their home, just like the leaves, grass, and dirt. They were there because they were part of the world in which I was sitting. As I fought off a panic attack, having seen a spider the size of a silver dollar heading my way (and it goes without saying that it was not really appropriate to kill them!), I was hit hard with the palpable knowledge that for my adopted mom, this would have been a comforting hiatus. She would have curled up in the pit, spiders and all, and gone to sleep for however long she was allowed to remain. There would have been no fear. It hit me how incredibly deep and enduring her quiet strength was. She was as rooted as an immense mountain and as immovable. The natural world held no fear for her, only solace and in this, she was stronger than I ever hope to be. I am a warrior. My strength is different. But it is not better. I came out of that pit humbled, awed, and moved to tears by the unassuming strength of my mother, strength she would not even recognize in herself as such.

The second part of my ordeal took place under the guidance of Frey. He spoke to my adopted mother and outlined a three day ordeal, also to take place at my friend's farm. This was designed, I believe, to break me of my arrogance and disregard of my farmer ancestors. Frey isn't just a God of the harvest and the land, but a God of the ancestors as well. During the first day of the ordeal, I was required to work the land. I stayed with a friend who is a farmer and during this day, I worked for several hours in his vegetable garden, working the soil by hand. The work was OK; the spiders not so much. My adopted mother and I were permitted to eat one handful of food for each hour worked. The food had to be comprised of grains, fruits, or vegetables only and had to be organic.

On the second day of the ordeal, both I and my adopted mother were required to completely fast, consuming only water. During that time, I worked several hours in my friend's vegetable garden. On the third day, there were no words given. Instead, I walked down to the field, the same field in which I had been buried for Nerthus. In the North end of this field stands a carved God-pole dedicated to Frey. There I made offerings to this God and listened to His words and His admonition: Remember. Remember what you have learned. Remember. My mother had also been given a lesson for me from Frey, which she had carefully written down.

Frey's Lesson: Day One

Peace is a terrible thing. It demands as many sacrifices and as much discipline as war. I, Ingvi Freyr, know this, I who will die in battle, I who can fight as fiercely as the best warriors, yet chose to become a hostage in the name of peace and for the sake of peace. No coward I, no pacifist, but yet I am a Peace-Keeper. That is what you must learn, my child. To be a warrior, you have to honor peace and peace-keepers with the same immediacy you feel toward war and warriors. You who know to give equal respect to Odin and Loki without falling into the trap of either/or should give equal respect to war and peace.

To be a farmer is like being a priest and as sacred: Farmers are the hallowers and priests of my blood. Every year, I submit to my throat being scythed, to my blood being spilled to hallow and fructify the earth so it may nourish the people. Farmers are the link between my blood and people being fed. Without the farmer, my blood is spilled for nothing, for working the soil is the only rite that will give power to my sacrifice. This is what you must learn, my child: that to be a priest you have to honor the farmer as your equal. Honor your farmer ancestors. If you miss a part, you miss the whole. I am Ingvi Freyr, Peace-Keeper and Fighter, and Farmer. Come to me on the third day.

During the first day, remember, a whole season will be contained in this one day, and in that time you are the link between My blood, the earth and the sustaining of your mother. In that time, she is your old mother, your pregnant wife, your small daughter—all that which you love and which depends upon your holy skill and strength at farming. If you fail, My blood is disregarded, desecrated by neglect. Earth lies fallow and your loved ones starve.

Day Two

Today contains all of the next season, and it will be hard because warriors rode through your land. They needed food so they took all they could, all you had worked for. They rode through the grain; they took your goat and most of your hens. They filled a sack with the contents of your storeroom. You have nothing. That is what war does to peace. That is partly why I became hostage. So work the soil, on an empty stomach, to salvage what you may of My blood and your effort so that you may not starve tomorrow. Today you will not be able to feed either yourself or your foster mother whom you love. That is what war does to peace.

(It is important to note that this was not an accusation. It was said without judgment. It was merely a statement of fact.)

Day Three

On the third day, no words were given. I was expected to open myself to Freyr directly and to receive His wisdom. One of the things that I learned, I who am so proud of my warrior's calling, was that war and peace, warriors and farmers are intertwined. Yes, the farmer is at the mercy of the warrior, but so too is the warrior at the mercy of the farmer. One must always eat, after all. I was reminded of the Napoleonic Wars when French forces tried to take Russia, and the Russian farmers starved the invading soldiers by burning their own fields as they retreated, giving the invading army no sustenance. That is the power of the farmer.

It seems for me that Vanaheim has become the central spiritual axis around which all the other ordeals revolve. Perhaps this is because finding the holy in the process of living, in embodiment, in the faulty nature of my own humanity, has been an incredibly difficult process for me. Perhaps because my warrior's arrogance is so great, perhaps because the places and ways in which I am broken and scarred require this often terrifying balm. I don't know. I only know that the Vanir have been immensely kind to me even as they have challenged and at times goaded me into knowledge. And I am grateful.

Ostara Ritual for Frey: Making Frith

Raven Kaldera

As Frey is a hostage among the Aesir, he speaks often for peace among them. His words have defused many a potential war and he is considered wise among them. At this time of the year we celebrate Frey's time in Asgard, where he feasts with the Aesir and works tirelessly for peace.

This ritual can be done with folk from both side of an argument who honestly want to create frith between them, perhaps done as a prelude to a serious discussion. It can also be done by a community that is worried about covert (or overt) trouble among their members, and wishes to bring frith to their people. It can be done as a solitary rite by someone who wishes this for a situation, a fight with an enemy (or friend) where people are taking sides, or even general work in the rest of the world. The only caveat is that frith must be honestly desired, and the ritualler must be willing to make compromises if the opponents are equally willing. Simply wanting things to be peaceful because everyone is doing things your way is not the answer.

The altar for this ritual should be draped with light blue and gold, and set with bowls filled with soil that has been warmed slightly in the oven. A single yellow candle, a pitcher of rainwater, a small bowl of seeds, a deer antler, and a horn of mead sit in the center. To begin, the officiant walks around the space with the deer antler, saying, "Hail and hallow, friend of frith, make this meeting fair and fertile." Then the officiant lights the candle, saying:

As your light shines forth in each of us,
Ingvi-Frey, may it shine forth this day.
You are a light in darkness,
A warm fire in the cold,
A torch that lights the way.

The officiant picks up the bowl of seeds, and says:

Wherever he walks, Ingvi spreads his seed
Of hope, of frith, of seeing the future
As a time of prosperity and not merely strife.
He plants his seed deep in the soil of possibility
And waits for it to sprout in even the strangest places.
We, too, are the carriers of Ingvi's seed.
We, too, can plant peace everywhere
And water it with attention, with care.
Take this seed now, hold it to your heart,
Imagine frith, and nest it into the welcoming soil.

*Each person comes forth and takes a seed, and pushes it down into a
bowl of soil. The seeds can be named, or the wishes may remain silent.
The officiant says:*

We water our hopes with tears,
We water our hopes with courage,
We water our hopes with will,
And frith will spring up in our footsteps.
Ingvi-Frey, frith-maker of Asgard,
Let our fears not rule us,
Let our words be eloquent,
Let our voices be calm,
Let our bodies not be knotted with anger,
Let us be an open channel
Of your finest qualities.

*Each person comes forth while the officiant speaks and pours a little
water onto the soil. Then the officiant takes the horn of mead and passes
it around, saying, "How will you work for frith?" Each person speaks of
how they will bring frith to some community that they belong to. The last
small bit of the mead is poured out into the soil, and the officiant says:*

Ingvi-Frey, be with us as we do your work,
Strengthen us and keep our hopes alight,
Frith-maker, Light-bringer,
Keeper of wisdom, mighty in solace,
Watch over us and the light we bear.

Ideally, if people are able to learn it, everyone should end by singing Groa's Fourth Charm. This is a shaman-song, one in a series of sung magical charms the ancient giantess Groa gave to her son Svipdag, and it is called "Foes To Friends":

You see my heart, and I am seen.
You hear my words, and I am heard.
You feel my fears, my foes, my flight,
You fathom deep my path and plight
And friendship steals across your sight,
And understanding steals your fight,
And we will reach across this road
And hand to hand we bring this right.

Ostara Recipes for a Frey Feast

Fava Beans in Bacon Sauce
Seawalker

Ingredients:
5 pounds fava beans
A handful of dried summer savory
4 bacon slices, diced
¼ cup flour
½ cup milk
Salt and pepper
Water

Remove the fava beans from their pods and boil them in salted water with a bit of the savory until they are tender but still slightly firm. Sauté the bacon until crisp and drain off the drippings. Stir flour into bacon drippings, then slowly add the milk, 1 cup of the cooking liquid, a pinch of salt and pepper, and the rest of the savory. Cook until slightly thickened and then stir in the cooked fava beans and serve.

Fennel in Cream Sauce
Raven Kaldera

Ingredients:
4 medium-sized bulb fennels
(in stores fresh fennel may be called anise to fino to finocchio)
3 tbsp. butter
¼ cup flour
½ cup cream
4 bacon slices, cooked crisp and crumbled
Pinch of salt
Pinch of nutmeg
Water

Trim the stems and any discolored parts from the fennel. Chop into slices, setting aside the feathery leaves and dicing them. Boil the root pieces in water with a pinch of salt for 15 minutes. When they are tender, drain and reserve the cooking liquid. In a saucepan, melt the butter and add the flour, stirring constantly. Gradually add the cream and 1 cup of the cooking liquid. Cook over medium heat, stirring constantly, until slightly thickened; add salt, pepper, and diced fennel leaves and cook for a minute more. Stir in the cooked fennel, put in its presentation dish, and sprinkle with the bacon bits.

Ham-Wrapped Endive
Seawalker

Ingredients:
4 Belgian endives
4 cooked lean ham slices
1 tbsp. lemon juice
3 tbsp. butter
¼ cup flour
1 ½ cups milk
½ cup shredded cheese, traditionally Emmentaler
Salted water

Cut a cone-shaped piece out of the base of each endive—that's the bitter part. Sprinkle endives with lemon juice, blanch them in salted water and drain. In a saucepan, melt the butter and stir in the flour. Cook, stirring constantly, for three minutes, but do not allow the mixture to discolor. Stir in the milk. Add the cheese, stirring over low heat until melted. Wrap each endive in a ham slice and place with the folded "seam" down in a baking dish. Pour the cheese sauce over the endives and bake ten minutes as 375 degrees until the surface of the sauce is browned. Serve immediately.

God of Love

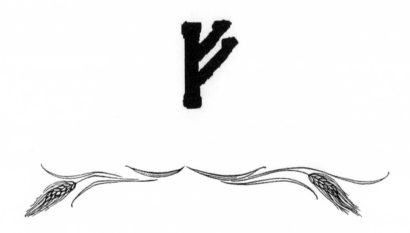

Prayer for the God of Love
Ari

Hail, Lord of the Beautiful Phallus!
Many scorn to call you so,
They cannot wrap their lips around
That ancient name, the tree that grows
From fertile earth to clouded sky,
But those of us who know you, know.

Hail, Lord of Divine Caress!
You grant us love with gentle laugh,
You show us ways to love that learn
To winnow treasure from the chaff,
You teach us that Lust can be clean,
You feed our bodies with your staff.

Prayer to Frey, God of Fertility
Michaela Macha

Frey, God of fertility,
I like to see the plants grow and thrive.
I enjoy animals being around—
the blackbird in the garden,
the cat in the yard, the lion on TV.
I know all life procreates,
And that for some privileged beings,
the act of procreating feels good—
And I know I can enjoy the good feeling
even if I choose not to procreate.
This option is a free gift that came with my body. More so,
it is a need you built in.
Perhaps, if I'd had a choice,
I'd have built myself otherwise,
but that's the way I am now.
Teach me to allow myself to feel at ease
when I feel lust stirring within me.
Teach me to accept it as natural and a sign of good health,
neither being ashamed of it,
nor making too big a fuss of it,
for it is a wonderful and ever-renewing gift
from Freya and from you.
In fact, enjoying my sexuality can bring me closer to you,
to understanding your ways and the mysteries of life.
Frey, God of body and mind, God of lust and love,
teach me to use your gift wisely.

Maypole
Jack Roe

The people dance
around Frey's Maypole
plunged into the earth our body
growing from the earth our body
to touch the sky
as the Vanic Lord ascends
to the realm of the sky
and down

he rises to the land of sky
falls to the land of earth
he falls again to the underworld
rises again to live once more
as the Maypole rises and falls
as the flesh pole rises and falls
as the grain rises and falls
as the sun rises and falls
with a shower of sparks
fireworks of pure living
streaming ribbons of color
seed of someday faraway fruit
fertilizing the future

we place our hands
on his Maypole
and take our oaths
on his sacredness
recognizing what is real
as the life between our thighs
as the life rising to our hearts
as the pleasure rising in our throats
to make us cry out

we recognize truth of the body
in his hands
a deeper truth than all the laws
written from the neck up

like a tree
he rises
and the people dance
for joy.

Frey of the Beautiful Phallus
Ari

Smile upon me, Rising God,
Fill me with your shaft of light,
Open me wide with joy.

It was a narrow time,
And I grew cramped
Living in severe straits
With no room for love.
I had near given up on love,
Actually, my hope was as thin
As string half worn through
By constant rubbing against stone.

Why bother? I could live alone
On canned peas and tuna,
On daily bulletins from friends,
On the occasional platonic embrace.
It was too hard anyway, the hunt,
The rejection, the fear, the trouble.
Too much trouble.

Smile upon me, Rising God,
Fill me with your shaft of light,
Open me wide with joy.

You came to me in the field
After everyone had gone to bed
With everyone else, except I alone.
Sulking and savoring my loneliness,
I sat self-satisfied and fatalistic
Until You came, laughing at me
And I knew I deserved it.

You turned me upside down,
Inside out, you caressed places
That had not been touched in years.
You were gentle, but you did not yield
Until I yielded, and then you were there.
It was all light and sound and beauty,
And afterwards I stared at stars
And made ready to get up the next morning
And see who there was to love.

Smile upon me, Rising God,
Fill me with your shaft of light,
Open me wide with joy.

Homestead
Raven Kaldera

His eyes are like the water in shaded duckponds,
Where frogs breed and tadpoles snatch the floating
Mosquito eggs, leafy bits floating green
On the surface. His gaze is the wind rippling
Through a field of barley, the drying sun
On the new-mown haybales, scented of vanilla.

This farm is old for this country, first the English
And then the Finns with their visiting tonttu
That we inherited with the sauna. My wife carries them
Beer and bread on late nights. Her maiden name is
Ingerson, some ancestor festival-got, spread before
The Golden One in a human body, gave her the gift
Of brewing. Gave me this land, through her.
I sink my hands in earth, manure black in the garden
Beneath the sprouting peas and beans.

His hair is amber on flax-strands, like my own
Used to be, before greying, but finer, gleaming.
Every waving head, awned and double-rowed,
Waves in His locks. His phallus is a tree, sturdy
And reliable, like the turning of the seasons.
There is no fragility, no petulance in His response,
No secret motivations. Just honest appreciation
And open warmth, an erection you could lean on
Like a staff in hard times.

"Is it in?" I ask my lover, knowing full well
But needing to hear it, breath caught, peeking
Between my mental fingers. He laughs, but it is
All right. If I had lived long ago, there would be
Bells on my hiked skirt, but the rest might be

Much the same. The grass tickles my cheek and the
Land-wight under me enjoys what I feel
Nearly as much as I do.

His laughter is the taste of cherries,
Tart on the tongue, sweet in the aftertaste,
Stone against your teeth as you spit out
New beginnings. His touch is solid as the ground
Beneath you, the slap of grass as you tumble down,
Rough on your shoulder like a hairy-chested lover.
All gods have contradictions, and his is the interplay
Of solid and ephemeral. When summer is upon you,
It feels like forever. I cannot convince myself
That each vibrant leaf will someday crumble.

The sheep graze content, already having forgotten
That one of their number went down to the bullet
This morning, already in pieces paper-wrapped
And freezer-ensconced. To create Life is to embrace
Death. Each carrot is John Barleycorn, who dies
For my hungers. Each cup of milk, of beer, is blessed.

His gentleness is the feel of dough
Beneath my hands as the powdered bodies
Of seeds that might have been sowed
Mix with the curd of milk taken from
My goat's udder, that nourished the kid I ate,
And water from my well, and living yeast
That will breathe my bread soft and high, and die
In heat and flames. Each loaf is a gift of submission.
His strength is the shell of a nut, cracked
With a grunt and the crunching of the meat,
Hard surrounding soft, easily opened.

Hazel, walnut, butternut. The leaves rustle

As I find the hard treasure in my fingers.
The walls of my old house are chestnut;
This place was once a grove, before white men
Came with saws and axes. Crosscut marks
Line the beams of my ceiling. Smooth and orange-brown,
I live surrounded by the bones of His bounty.

His courage is like the plowed earth, yielding and soft
And yielding is where the bravery truly comes in—
The moment when the black-robed woman stands
Before Him; see how He kneels with such serenity
And lifts His chin to make it easier
For her, the final stroke. Hair spilled into the grain
As the last of his breath passes, but tomorrow
There will be life, and life is worth it.

You see, He says, this is how Sacrifice should be done.
Not grudging, not grumbling. Not like you do it.
Lift your head and welcome the stroke.
Remember all the reasons for it. So He tells me,
And I feel His smile. But I am human, imperfect.
I fight and wrench myself. Perhaps next year
I will watch his sacrifice again, and this time perhaps
I will be able to find in myself a hundredth of His grace.
If not then, the year after. He never shirks His task.

His soul is a seed, so much growing from so little.
How can such a tiny thing encompass so much?
I am struck by the beauty of blood
Splashed on the sheaf of grain, scarlet on gold
And this is his Mystery.

My Fulltrui Is Frey The Bold

Michaela Macha

My fulltrui is Frey the bold,
the Lord of land and fields.
His people say the staff he holds
is strong and never yields.
As Yggdrasil is tall and proud,
as Irminsul unending,
Frey's staff is standing straight and stout
and never will be bending.

My fulltrui is Frey the fair,
who makes the plants to grow.
His fountain rises in the air
and brings a fertile flow.
As waterfalls from mountains pour
and geysers reach the sky,
Frey's fountain splashes evermore
and never will run dry.

My fulltrui is Frey, the Lord
of peasants and of farms.
They say he gave away his sword,
but he has other arms.
He fights with grace and prowess,
and though his peace is steady,
for giant and for giantess
his antler's always ready.

My full-tru-i is Frey the bold, the Lord of land and fie-lds. His

peo-ple say the staff he holds is strong and ne-ver yie-lds. As

Ygg-dra-sil is tall and proud, as Ir-min-sul un-end-ing, Frey's

staff is stand-ing straight and stout, and ne-ver will be bend-ing. My...

The melody is from "The Beehive", printed in "Pills to Purge Melancholy", a collection of popular English songs, published 1698-1720 by Thomas Durfey. This poem is © Michaela Macha in the Common Domain and may be freely distributed provided it remains unchanged, including copyright notice and this License.

Beltane Ritual for Frey: Sacred Pleasure

Raven Kaldera

For this ritual, you will need a carved wooden phallus. It can be life-sized (if generous) or larger-than-life. The base can be decorated with ribbons, or twin bags filled with unshelled nuts if you wish. The altar should be draped with green, and leafy boughs laid upon it. A bowl of mead should be present for an offering, and a bowl of honey as well. A pile of wreaths of flowers and leaves should be made beforehand, in many sizes, so that all attendees can take one.

To begin, the officiant beats the drum and calls out:

Hail to the Spring Lord in his greenery!
Ingvi, we see you leap forth in the new shoots,
The saplings, the ferns, each uncurling leaf!
You are eager to reach for the sky,
As your sacred cock rises from the earth,
The earth your body, the earth our bodies,
We feel life rise within us!

The officiant holds up the wooden phallus and says:

As oaths for life are taken on the Maypole,
On Frey's pole we take oaths of the body.
Take it, hold it in your hands, and tell us
What you will do for your own body,
How you will show love for it,
How you will hold sacred the tides of love.

The phallus is passed around, and each person speaks about what they will do to release inhibitions, or pay more attention to their own sexual needs, or purge themselves of baggage, or whatever they are moved to say when holding Frey's pole. When all have spoken, the officiant takes the bowl of honey and passes it around, saying:

Taste of the honey of the Golden God
And speak of the sweetest thing in your life,
And offer Him your gratitude.

The people each taste of the honey with their fingers, and speak of the sweetest thing in their lives and why they are grateful for it. The officiant then takes the pile of wreaths and places them, one at a time, over the phallus. The officiant then says, "Come and wreathe yourselves in the green of spring, and accept Frey's blessing on you." Each comes forth and takes a wreath from the pile, placing it on their head or that of someone else, until all are wreathed. The officiant pours out the mead onto the earth, saying, "As you give us sweetness, so we return it to you." Then the officiant calls out:

In the name of the Golden God of Love,
Go forth and give each other pleasure!
But remember the Earth on which you lie,
Remember to give back what has been taken,
And send some of your sacred pleasure
Back into the Earth that shaped your flesh.

With much cheering, the people go off to give each other pleasure. If there is a group sex rite, the wooden phallus should be passed around during the sex, held by different people as they play, in order to make it an offering to Frey.

A note on "anonymous sex rituals": There is a lot of idealistic Pagan literature, fictional and nonfictional, about sacred group sex rites where people openly share their bodies with a variety of individuals during a ritual period. We have found that these rituals almost never go the way that they are planned. Occasionally, when the Gods smile on us, they can spontaneously reach the kind of body-centered, easy, uncomplicated ecstasy that everyone hopes for. Most of the time, however, they end to result in discomfort for a lot of people. Modern humans are, for the most part, still very hung up when it comes to sex.

If you expect a varied group of people to get it together and start having sex with other people, including people they hardly know, it can go wrong very quickly. Some people will mill about, wanting to do something but not being able to bring themselves to make a move and perhaps look stupid, or get rejected. Some people will come on too hard to someone who doesn't want them, and the rejection will get ugly and be detrimental to the atmosphere. Some people will take gentle rejection too seriously and flee weeping. People with poor boundaries will let themselves be pressured by the occasion into sex they don't want with people they don't want it with, and will either eventually flee weeping, or there will be all sorts of accusatory repercussions later. Someone who thought that they were more polyamorous than they actually are will have a meltdown upon seeing their lover with someone else. Even if several people do get it on together, there will still be a percentage of the unwanted milling about and feeling miserable. Frankly, most modern people cannot be trusted with the gift of Frey that is indiscriminate love and pleasure in the body. There's too much baggage around it, too much pain and inhibition from our various social upbringings.

In general, we've found that it's better to reserve such rituals for a small and intimate group of people who know each other well and have all had sexual adventures together with each other, so that there will be no surprises. In the case of a less intimate gathering, one can encourage couples (or larger groups) who are already intimate to go off with each other (and provide comfortable and private spaces for them), but there needs to be a meaningful alternative ritual for those who don't have partners, or find themselves not up to being sexual. This should be something better than just having them drum for the other people's lovemaking, unless this is something that they all decide spontaneously that they are moved to do. One possibility is for them to focus their energy on the earth and drum sexual energy into it; another might be to have a guided meditation that brings them into Frey's presence and allows them to ask him a question about the subject. Yet another option is to have a group massage, or have a few volunteer massagers who are willing to do nonsexual but loving massage for people, in a way that helps them to get in touch with their bodies without creating pressure or awkwardness. Whatever you choose, remember that Frey wants people to be as joyous as possible, not uncomfortable, whatever that entails. If at all possible, no one should feel penalized for not living in a perfect world.

Beltane Recipes for a Frey Feast

Pork Cutlets with Marjoram
Seawalker

Ingredients:
One large boneless pork loin
Salt and freshly ground black pepper
Whole-grain mustard
5 tablespoons lard or butter
1 slices onion
1 peeled and diced apple
4 tbsp. chopped fresh marjoram

Cut the pork loin into inch-thick cutlets and pound them a little. Sprinkle them with a pinch of salt and pepper and spread them with mustard. In a skillet, heat half the lard or butter and start to brown the onion and apple slices. Add the rest of the lard or butter, brown the pork cutlets on both sides (non-mustard side first), reduce the heat, cover, and cook for 3 minutes. Then sprinkle them with the marjoram, cover again, and cook for 2 more minutes or until they are thoroughly cooked.

Cream of Chervil Soup
Seawalker

Ingredients:
3 cups pork stock
¼ cup butter
¼ cup flour
1 cup milk
1/3 cup cream
Salt and white pepper
1 cup chopped fresh chervil

Melt butter in a saucepan and add flour, stirring constantly. Stir in the stock, then the milk, then the cream, then add the salt and white pepper. Stir for 5 more minutes, then add the chervil to the soup and cook only 1 minute more. It should dye the soup a lovely green. Don't overcook the chervil—it will lose its color and flavor.

Frey's Pigs
Tchipakkan

Ingredients:
7 oz. almond paste
1 cup powdered sugar
2 cups ground almonds
Pinch salt
1 jigger rum
1 egg white
A few drops yellow or red food coloring

Dice the almond paste and knead with the other ingredients. In Europe there are little molds which can be used to form these into little pigs. As our children may not care for marzipan the way our ancestors did, you may wish to keep the pigs small, or even leave out the egg white. Without the egg, wrapped marzipan will keep almost indefinitely. They are adorable in pink, but you can also gild the pig, as Frey's mount Gullinbursti was said to be gold. Of course marzipan can also be formed into almost any shape or tinted almost any color to make whatever you like. But I like to give "good little children" a golden pig.

Light-Bringer

Prayer for the Light-Bringer
Ari

Hail to the God of the Spark Inside,
Enduring warmth that ever hides
Where we forget that deep it lies
Till sorrow sees its sudden rise.
You are the light beneath the skin,
You are the dawn that rises in
The east, direction of the mind.
You are the comfort that I find
When I finally let go of care
And all the daily woes that wear
My will and heart to shreds and tatters—
You tell me that these things don't matter,
That only Love survives the pass,
That desolation never lasts.
Hail Frey, from whom I ever learn
That in my hearth, the embers burn.

A Discipline of Optimism

Joshua Tenpenny

> *"The Happiness of every Man depends More upon the State of*
> *his own Mind, than upon any one External Circumstance:*
> *Nay, more than upon All External Things put together."*
> *– Murray's English Reader, 1828.*

Some people say we create our own reality. I don't know if that is true, but certainly we create our own *experience* of reality. The meanings we attach to events have a greater and more lasting impact on us than the events themselves. What I have learned from Frey is that it is possible to take joy in each moment of life, no matter how painful. We are all still growing and learning, so we often find we are not strong enough or whole enough to reach for that joy. It may be so far beyond our present capabilities that in the moment we cannot fathom how it could be so, but the *possibility* always exists. Life involves pain, it is just the way of things, but suffering is never mandatory. Frey assures me of this. For a given person, in a given situation, suffering may be unavoidable, but it is never strictly mandatory. *Always choose joy*, he said to me. Whenever possible, whenever you can see even the smallest glimmer of a choice, choose joy. It wasn't a command. It was an invitation. It was permission.

Choosing joy is a skill. It can be learned, and with practice, you can get better at it. Some may have more of an aptitude than others, but while I don't know for certain that everyone could effectively learn these skills, I'm confident a great many people can. You don't have to be a naturally optimistic person to do this. I certainly wasn't. Like many people, I was drawn to Frey because his experience of joy and light was something I needed to learn, not something I already had. For a while, it felt as if I was carefully protecting a tiny spark of joy against the crushing darkness within me and around me. Now connecting to that joy feels more like clearing the clouds away from the sun, rather than kindling a fire from nervously guarded coals. The more you apply these skills, the easier it becomes.

Practice continually on small inconsequential things, and over time, you'll find that you can apply these skills to progressively larger issues. Practice is essential. You wouldn't try to run a marathon with no preparation, then decide you just aren't cut out for running based on that one failed attempt. So if you are in the aftermath of some great personal tragedy, it is not reasonable to expect to master this all at once, or to fault yourself for being unable to. While it is theoretically possible to learn how to choose joy under such circumstances, it requires such a radical shift of consciousness that few people can manage it. So start small, when you are not in a state of acute crisis, and you stand a much better chance of making progress. If you would like to experiment with how a discipline of optimism can change your life, here are a handful of practices to try.

Practice One: Let go of suffering.

Most of us face small challenges in the course of our day that are well within our capabilities to handle, but we let them get to us anyway. Have you ever said something like, "I have the right to be angry at her!" Certainly, you do. You have that right. But no matter how badly she hurt you, you are never *obligated* to be angry at her. Perhaps at that moment, you are so immersed in that anger that you can't see your way clear of it, but eventually the acute pain-driven anger will subside, and you'll be able to get a little perspective on the issue. At some point, your personal resources will be greater than the anger, and you will be capable of releasing that anger. Then you get to choose. Will you remain angry? Will you continue to suffer over this wrong? Or will you let it go? Just asking yourself these questions can begin to loosen the grip the emotion has on you and the grip you have on the emotion. If you think the other person doesn't "deserve" forgiveness, please understand that your anger and resentment will cause you infinitely more suffering than it will ever cause them. If you must put your energy into the situation, put your energy into fixing the problem, not into feeding your anger. It is the same for sorrow, for grief, for jealousy. When you are able to let them go, do it! Don't try to force the feelings away, just stop holding on to them. Stop identifying with the emotions, and realize you are not obligated to feel them. Stop choosing to suffer when you don't have to.

Practice Two: Don't encourage failure.

Even if you don't consider yourself a pessimistic person, you may find you respond to the minor annoyances of life with an ironic sense of humor that identifies unfortunate circumstances as more likely than fortunate ones. "There was a big pile of dog poop in the middle of the sidewalk, and I was wearing my new shoes, so *of course* I stepped right in it!" If pressed, most people would say they don't "mean anything" by statements like this, that they are just joking, and they don't *actually* believe they are statistically more likely to step in poop when wearing new shoes. Comments like this, whether said aloud or internally, can be a way of releasing tension over an upsetting situation. However, recognize that you are sending yourself repeated messages that the more important something is to you, the more likely it is to go wrong. Stopping this habit can be a way of focusing your attention on maintaining a more genuinely optimistic frame of mind.

Practice Three: Enjoy ordinary things.

Throughout your day, look for things you usually don't take much notice of, and deliberately try to enjoy them. Things don't have to be extraordinary to be enjoyable. It isn't as if you need to save up your enjoyment for a special occasion. In fact, try thinking of it the opposite way. What if at any random moment, you had to pick something—anything—in your present environment to enjoy? Can you find something? Some object that is nice to look at. Some pleasant sensation. Some person you can cultivate positive emotions towards. If this prompts you to add more enjoyable things to your daily routine, wonderful, but also try to enjoy what is already there. Challenge yourself to expand your concept of what is enjoyable. If the weather is even remotely pleasant, can you think to yourself that it is a beautiful day? Can you enjoy the completely ordinary sandwich you have for lunch? Reject "gourmet consciousness" which only enjoys the best of the best, and enjoy the normal good things of everyday life. I don't mean to encourage a lazy "close enough, good enough" mentality, with lower and lower standards. There is value in pursuing perfection, but you can still enjoy the countless imperfect things you encounter along the way.

Practice Four: Look for the reason. Look for the lesson.

Sometimes challenging things happen to us for a reason. They help us grow. They point us in the right direction when we were headed the wrong way. They show us something about ourselves. They give us compassion for others. Sometimes we struggle with the pain of life's natural transitions and limitations. Sometimes a terrible thing just happens with no reason, and it isn't about us at all. No matter what the "real" reason is, whether there is one reason or twenty or none at all, when you are faced with a situation that brings up negative emotions, speculate about how you would feel if these same circumstances were due to some beneficial reason that is not immediately obvious. The practice here isn't to attempt to discern the reason, but to open your mind and heart to the possibility that a reason might exist. This can help you to understand, on a deep intuitive level, that your emotional response to most situations is based on your interpretation of the reasons and meanings behind a situation, and is not an unavoidable direct consequence of that situation. I'm reluctant to retell the old story about the man whose horse ran away, but if you can think about times when a seemingly bad situation really did work out for the best, this can help get you into the right mindset. You can also look at the situation and ask yourself, "If there was a lesson here, if this situation were arranged to teach me something, what might that be?" or "What would have to change within me for this situation not to bother me as much?" Even if this circumstances wasn't divinely arranged as some kind of learning experience for you, you can still take the opportunity to grow and change and learn.

Practice Five: Find someone who benefits.

If some circumstance doesn't work out well for you, try thinking lovingly about how someone else might have benefitted from your misfortune. This one is a tricky one, so don't force it. Just allow yourself to be open to the idea. Start small. Perhaps the person you let in line in front of you at the bakery got the last chocolate cake. Can you find a way to genuinely share joy in their good fortune? Imagine what it would be like if your immediate instinctive response was to share their joy rather than thinking of your own loss. It is easier when it is someone we care about who benefits, so some spiritual traditions suggest acting as if everyone you encounter is your mother, or your child, or your beloved. If you develop a loving compassion towards all people, you can cultivate this feeling towards complete strangers.

Practice Six: Bless the people who trouble you.

When someone does something hurtful, they are often acting out of their own pain and damage. Can you have compassion for them, rather than anger? Can you imagine being in a situation where you'd do something similar to what they have done? It is often circumstances of desperation, fear, and need that lead to hurtful actions. Can you pray for this person? Can you pray that they find relief from whatever has troubled them, and that they find the strength to act with compassion despite their challenging circumstances? When faced with someone whose actions are so hateful that we cannot relate to their motivations, can you feel a genuine sorrow for this person's situation, and a sincere wish that they find some way to a happy, fulfilled place where such actions are as unthinkable to them as they are to you? Remember that you can act against hateful actions without joining in the hate.

These are just a few suggestions. They are tools, not rules. If you are facing a situation that overwhelms your personal resources and you aren't able to approach it with any optimism, don't feel guilty about it and don't give up. It is okay to be imperfect! I recently faced a situation that was way too much for me to handle. I tried to have a good attitude, but I was just miserable the whole time. Afterwards, I prayed about it. I apologized to Frey for failing at my discipline of optimism. The feeling I got was something like "Don't be silly. This is for your own benefit, not mine, so why apologize to me?" Again I was reminded that this is not a command. It is an invitation. So if this path calls to you, give it a try.

What Shall We Sing to Frey

Michaela Macha
(Inspired by: Rig Veda Hymn XLIII. Rudra.)

What shall we sing to Frey, most strong,
most bounteous, excellently wise,
that shall be dearest to his heart?
That Gerd may grant the grace of Frey to our folk, our kin,
our cattle and our progeny:
That Thor and Freya and Frey may remember us,
yea, all the Gods with one accord.

To Frey, Lord of Sacrifice, of healing and well-being,
we pray for joy and health and strength;
May he grant health to our steeds, fertility to family,
to men, to women, and to kine.
He shines in splendour like the sun,
refulgent as bright gold is he,
the good, the best among the Gods.
O Frey, make us great by your glory,
grant us renown for right deeds.
Let not troubles hinder us to honor
the Blot-God as shares with us his strength.
Frey! With head, and heart, and loin we serve you,
your children, immortal in your service,
at the highest place of holy law.

Bringer of Light
Jon Norman

I've spent a lot of my life in the darkness. Ingvi-Frey came into my life, and brought me light. For a large portion of my life I struggled with mental illness and as I got older, addiction almost destroyed me. I grew up with alcoholic/addict parents who were never able to give me the love I needed. I found comfort and filled the emptiness inside of me with food and later, with self-injurious behavior, alcohol, and drugs. I felt alone for a very long time. As a child, I didn't have many friends. I was often the target of bullying and harassment because of my weight and sexual orientation. I struggled silently for what seemed like an eternity. I was 16 or 17 when my parents divorced, and I chose to stay with my father. A couple of years later, he overdosed on heroin.

After my father died, my own drug use significantly escalated. I had never really thought I was a drug addict, but I started doing things that I had sworn to myself I would never do. I had seen how drugs had affected my parents and so many other people in my life, but the pain I was experiencing was so unbearable, I didn't know how to deal with it. I started smoking crack cocaine and using heroin nasally, and I "progressed" to using cocaine and heroin intravenously, in combination. Over the next couple of years, I did everything I could to get and stay high. I lied, stole, and pretty much sold myself. By the end of my addiction, not only had I lost all of my friends, all of my material possessions, and all of my self-respect, but I had lost all hope for the future and all faith in the Gods.

On October 6, 2006, while in a state of cocaine-induced psychosis, I attempted suicide. I had come to the point where I sincerely did not want to live. For the first time in my life, I was not at all afraid of death. In active addiction, I had many close calls with death, I had even been brought to the point of trying to take my own life, but this was different. When I woke up from my suicide attempt, I heard a voice saying "You had to die for the addict to die, you had to die to be reborn" ... and for once, I actually felt OK. It was like I felt peaceful, for the first time in years. It only lasted for a few seconds before the reality of what had happened set in, but I realized at that moment that I was given another chance at life.

I was in the Intensive Care Unit for a few days, then in a psychiatric hospital for a couple weeks, then an inpatient rehabilitation center. While I was in rehab, I started to pray. I hadn't really prayed in a long time, aside from asking for material things or to get me out of whatever trouble I was in. I had to learn to pray ... I started to give thanks for the few things I still had in my life and to ask for the strength to stay clean. It felt like I was doing the right thing. I still didn't have any real faith, but the staff kept telling us about how important it was to have a Higher Power. I tried to pray, everyday. For some reason, I felt the need to reach out to Frey ... I prayed from him to bring light into my life.

Slowly, I made progress, and I eventually went home. I took the suggestions I was given, and started the aftercare program I was referred to—I actually kept showing up—and doing it clean! I kept praying ... in the morning, giving thanks for the new day and for the chance I had been given to live, and asking for the strength and courage I needed to make it through the day, without using. When I went to bed, I expressed my gratitude for the aid I had been given throughout the day, for all of the blessings in my life. I prayed for the guidance, strength, and courage that I would need on my path. I also use a set of prayer beads at least twice a day, immediately upon waking up, and right before going to sleep. I continued to pray to Frey, asking him to brighten my dark life.

Soon after I got home strange things started to happen. At first I barely noticed them, but everywhere I looked, I saw things that reminded me of Frey: every e-mail list I was on was discussing him, and whenever I opened a book, it was always to a page about Frey. Everywhere I looked I would see Ingwaz runes— in trees, on the ground, in patterns of wallpaper, and when I'd close my eyes and meditate. The Ing-rune would almost seem to jump out of my bag of runes. At first I brushed it off as coincidence, but it continued and got even more extreme, everywhere I looked I would see things that would scream "Frey!".

I kept praying, I tried to reach out to Ingvi-Frey, I offered him gifts, and prayer. I was very skeptical about this, because I had no faith, still. I wanted to believe, but I had been hurt so much, rejected, and abandoned ... I felt so empty inside. Then it happened. Frey came into my life as a feeling—a feeling of pure, unconditional love. He wrapped around me, and filled me, and made me complete. For once, in my life, I didn't feel alone, the void inside of me was filled, and I knew that there was hope for me.

I had been beat up and knocked down by life, I had such a resentment towards the Gods, I wanted to deny this experience at first. I didn't want to believe that it really could have been Frey, a God, actually caring about me and wanting to help me. It started to get hard to deny. The little coincidences and signs started happening even more often. The feelings were present a lot. Every time I started to doubt, I would see or hear or feel something that would reassure me.

I had a lot of hard times ... I suffered from severe insomnia throughout the first six months of my sobriety. I had intense cravings. I was very much alone. I had to give up all of my old friends, so I had no one. I would sit in my room, alone for hours and think about using, sometimes crying, or screaming. I would pray ... and every time, I would feel a little better. Not once did I go out and get high.

As I continued to progress in my recovery, I had more and more faith that I would be given what I needed to stay clean; that it was not an impossible task. I made it through a lot of very hard times. I prayed for help, and was given many blessings. I believe that people were put in my life when I needed them. I was going through a long, hard stretch. The lack of supportive people in my life was starting to take its toll on me. I prayed for support, and the next day I was "thrown" into a very unexpected service position. As a result of it, I was immediately surrounded by tons of supportive people, some of who became important parts of life.

I pray multiple times a day. I use prayer beads in the morning and at night, and use other less structured prayers. I give gifts, because I have been given me so much, and it's the least I can do. Through meditation and utiseta, I have been able to connect with Frey on a deeper level. I take time out to just listen; this has been an important part of our relationship. A lot of times the messages don't come as spoken words, but as thoughts, pictures, or feelings. Sometimes I have no idea what He's trying to tell me, and it takes time to understand the message. Patience is very important, and it is something I'm trying to learn.

I've been clean for a year, now. There is no way I could have done it without Frey's love and support. He has given me more gifts than I ever thought possible. He has truly brought light into my life.

Lammas Night
Joshua Tenpenny

I walked up the steps and cautiously opened the door. "Come in, lad!" he boomed, with a bright, jolly voice that I tried to let soothe my nervousness. I set my bottle down on the table, and climbed onto the bed where he sat. For weeks I had let my enthusiasm about this evening obscure every other thought. Now that it arrived, I was so worried about doing something awkward that I could barely think about this sex I had been so eagerly anticipating. That is what I was invited here for. The shaman-priest had called Frey into his body for the ritual, and I am one of the offerings. Like the beer, and the bread, and the prayers and songs. It never occurred to me that it would have anything to do with me personally.

Frey looked at me with a big smile and chided, "Did you think I'd want nothing but your body, lad? Did you think I'd have nothing to say to you?" I stammered that I didn't know, which was the closest thing to a verbal response I was able to give the whole evening.

He cheerfully continued, with an intensity that was almost conspiratorial, but always with the bright, laughing eyes. "You're working with my sister now. She has many things to teach you ... but there are things she does not know! ... What *I* know is the love that endures—love that is bound to the land. You understand this. Yes... Yes!" And I saw Freya's love, the ephemeral bliss and timeless beauty, against his love, binding husband and wife securely to their home and to each other.

But there was more. "You and I are more alike than you think. I know about sacrifice. Ha! Yes, I *know* about sacrifice." And I saw him as the pure golden god who is cut down at his height, approaching death not with a grim acceptance or dutiful obligation but a big smile and that ever-present erection, celebrating even this aspect of life. And more... "I also know what it is like to love one of *that* blood. There could be no Asa bride for me. No, I needed someone dark, someone wild. And I too know what it is to willingly be completely defenseless for that love." I recalled the irony of this gorgeous god desperately courting a fierce giantess who scorned his beautiful home and people, accepting only when he gave his sole weapon as a bride-price... and then my defenselessness against my own lover and his murky twisted Jotun bloodlines.

When I managed to hold his gaze it was mesmerizing. He spoke in plain words, but what he communicated was more than the words. As he spoke it cued up thoughts, memories and images in my head, crystallizing them, giving form to what I knew but had no words for. Each time he explained something and said, "You know this. Yes? Yes!" he made that knowledge more real. It was if he was evoking knowledge already within me rather than teaching me something new. Afterwards it was all so clear that I couldn't imagine that there had ever been a time when I didn't understand these things.

"Give me a drink, lad!" We shared a generous quantity of mead, and then, finally, was the sex. The activities needn't be detailed here, but I will say that it while it was a glorious experience, there was a distressingly ambivalent component to it for me. A bright light casts a dark shadow, and in comparison to his brilliance I felt acutely self-conscious of my flaws. I was embarrassed to feel so neurotic during what I had thought would be a purely joyful experience for me. Secretly, I felt I had failed in some way. I didn't talk about this aspect of it for a few years. I thought it would confuse the telling of what was such an overwhelmingly positive experience, and it was so difficult for me to admit.

Then I heard other people report having this type of response to Frey and to the other Bright Gods, and I saw that same mixture of awe and shame in their eyes. It became plain to me that this was a natural response rather than my peculiar failure. We are all flawed in some way, and there is no sense in feeling bad about it. Work on improving yourself, certainly, but don't be ashamed of where you are at in your development compared to where you think you ought to be. To experience pure joy, you need to be exactly who you are, and be right here, right now. There is no success or failure, just the experience. I'm still trying to learn this.

Afterwards, he put his mouth to my chest and blew into my heart, and then into my mouth, saying "Let this be a light in the darkness. Because there *will* be darkness." That was what he left me with. That was his gift to me. I can, at any time, no matter my situation, call up that golden glow of being in his presence by focusing intently on that light. If I truly want it, I can breathe on that tiny spark and kindle it into a bright flame that casts aside all other feelings.

It took some time for the effect of this to really sink in. It meant that I had to admit to myself how reluctant I really am to part with my fear and hatred and anger. Part of my personal spiritual path is to love everyone, unconditionally. That is an easy thing to say, but deeply transformative to actually do. I had struggled for years with being unable to feel any kind of love for certain people, but after receiving this Light, I know that I am not actually unable, just unwilling. Even though I know better, part of me cannot accept that withholding my love hurts me immeasurably more than it hurts the other person. Part of me still needs to deem people worthy or unworthy of my love, but the sun shines on the just and unjust man alike. To let love pour forth from you is to be like the sun. Unconditional love does not condone evil any more than it rewards good, because it is *truly* unconditional. It is not a matter of "lowering the bar" so far that even the most reprehensible individual seems to have something lovable about them. It dispenses with the bar entirely. It is that radical.

Many of the folks I work with spiritually are heavily involved in ordeal work and other dark aspects of spirituality. They can be very dismissive of the "bright" stuff, as if that is for the "fluffy bunny" pagans, the wide eyed blissed-out folks, the ignorant and naïve, or perhaps the few lucky innocents who have been sheltered from the real world and spared its suffering. There is a pervasive idea among them that the brightness is an illusion and pain is what is real, that pleasure is shallow and the ordeal is the only way to the deeper mysteries. Most don't really understand that going up is just as hard as going down; it is just hard in different ways. It means knowing the loss and pain of life and seeing it as part of the joy, loving and embracing it all as the beauty of embodied existence. It means sacrificing your every hatred, and laying down your every weapon in order to love fully and without reservation. It means surrendering to the unknown, not just willingly, but joyfully. That is Frey's lesson to me, and the example I will always strive for.

Finding Frey
Svartesol

I found Him in the grove
under the shadow of the trees
In the leaves, in the grass,
rustling in the breeze
I found Him in the wild
running with the deer
I heard His call to follow Him
and ran into my fear

I fell through a hole
I found Him in the mound
in the darkness and the silence,
swallowed up by the ground,
eaten by the worms—
bones dissolve into dust
He took away my old life
and its stains and its rust

From the Earth, born anew—
then I found Him in the wain
He asked me to sit beside Him
and start over again
His chariot took us
down a long and winding road
To bless homes and hearts
and the fields of gold

In thanks for His help
a temple was raised
I built a place for Him
to ever be praised
I share my home with Him

And offer up my days
To the God of my World
I hail You, Ing-Frey

Skidbladnir

Shannon Graves

When I knew I was trapped
with no way out of the rabbit's race
until the child was grown enough
to stand on her own
I called to the golden god
he promised me freedom
if I sacrificed, if I waited
for blessed are those who sacrifice
for love of those in need
so I wrote his rune of promise
on a slip of paper and folded it
into a ship in the palm of my hand
I tucked it into my pocket
wore it next to my meager wealth
a promise held, a promise kept
until it was time to fly.

The Holy Twins

Gudrun of Mimirsbrunnr

Twins were a common sacred theme in ancient Indo-European mythology. They are found throughout the paths of those peoples, from Greece (Artemis and Apollo, Helen and Clytemnestra, Castor and Pollux), from the Celts (the twins of Macha, left over from a number of IE "horse twins"), from India (the Ashvinis), the Lithuanians (the Asvieniai), the Latvians (the Dieva Deli), the Romans (Romulus and Remus), and the proto-Germanic peoples (the Alcis, or twins of the sacred grove).[1] It seems that the concept of two children born at once from a single womb was a sacred event, a sign of abundance and an omen that the Gods had blessed the people.

While there is technically no mention of the Norse Gods Frey and Freyja being twins, it would be contrary to the entirety of the Indo-European culture that bore them into this world if they were not. They function very much as sacred twins in this cosmology, the way that Artemis and Apollo function in the Greek pantheon—and, like them, they are both associated with light-bringing. However, where the Greek twins are celestial, the Norse twins are very earthy and associated with fertility and love. Their names—which are really titles, *Lord* and *Lady*—are somewhat difficult to etymologize, but their seem to be two likely possibilities, much debated. One is that the term comes from the IE word *per*, meaning first or forward, which became the Proto-Germanic *frawan*, or chief.[2] Another possibility is that the word comes from the Proto-Indo-European *Pieheh, which means "beloved". this word was the root for the names of several love deities and "love concepts", including the Sanskrit *Priya* and

---

[1] Ward, Donald: *The Divine Twins*, Folklore Studies, No. 19, Univ. Calif. Press, Berkeley, 1968

[2] Watkins, Calvert. *The American Heritage Dictionary of Indo-European Roots*. Boston, Houghton-Mifflin, 2000.

Prajapati, the Hittite *Purulli*, the Albanian *Perendi*, the Bohemian
Priye, the Persian *Peri* (elf), and the Greek *Priapos* which was
Latinized to *Priapus*. At some point, a whole host of P-words
were slurred into F-words by the Germanic branch of the IE
languages, which is why we have *father* instead of *pater*, *fish* instead
of *pisces*, and Frey/Freyja instead of Priapos or Priya.[3]

As children of an Earth Mother and a Sea Father, they are
manifestations of food abundance on both land and sea—very
important for a culture developed in a place of many coastlines and
not much fertile land. Njord's fish were as important as Nerthus's
crops, and by creating Divine Twins between them, it was assured
that both food sources would function as a bountiful and
interdependent whole. The attributes of both fertility and being
saviors at sea are part of the repeating characteristics of IE sacred
twins.[4] While both twins were probably invoked at various times
of the year, Freyja seems to be more associated with springtime
while Frey with his Sacrificial Corn King aspect appears later in
the year. This would posit them at opposite ends of the harvest
process, with Freyja inspiring the seed and flower, and Frey
embodying the cutting-down.

Another set of repeating characteristics among twins is
association with the Sun—sometimes through a solar/lunar pair,
sometimes through twin brothers who are siblings of the Sun
Maiden or Dawn Goddess. In the case of the Norse twins there is
no lunar theme, but a sort of slurring of the Sun Maiden/Dawn
Goddess with a brother ... and again, I emphasize "of a sort".
Neither Frey nor Freyja are direct solar embodiments per se, that
role being taken by Sunna, but they are both generally conceived
of as "golden" deities and are associated with amber and honey,

[3] Mallory, James P.; Adams, Douglas P. (2006), *Oxford Introduction to
Proto-Indo-European and the Proto-Indo-European World*, London:
Oxford University Press
[4] Michael Shapiro, *Neglected Evidence of Dioscurism (Divine Twinning) in
the Old Slavic Pantheon*, JIES 10 (1982)

both solar substances. The gold of the Sun and the gold of the grainfields reflect each other, in many historical cultures. The Norse Twins are not the Sun in the sky, but the sunlight that touches the leaves of food plants, which can be conceived of as a separate connection.

In some divine twin mythemes, the twins actually have separate paternities (even though they are born at the same time) which determine their separate fates. This is reflected in the myth of Castor and Pollux, where the divine son of Zeus remains in the heavenly realm while the mortal son dies and must be rescued by his brother. While Njord seems to be firmly the father of both the Vanic twins, Frey dies and is returned to the earth each year, while Freyja does not, echoing the Dioscuri theme. In a sense, one twin ascends while the other descends. On the other hand, Frey is happily married (after a tumultuous courtship) while Freyja is either portrayed as belonging to no one or recently widowed. Her fruitless search for her lost husband may be seen as her own turn at the underworld journey, where Frey rules above with his bride.

One of the most difficult and uncomfortable themes between the Vanic siblings (for modern people, anyway) is the idea that they are sexual with each other. In the Lokasenna, Loki accuses Frey and Freyja of having sex together in public where the other gods could see, and makes scatological references to Freyja's behavior. Njord speaks up for his children and defends their practice as being no shame at all, which may be the echo of an old myth of divine incest coming up against the newer Christian thought, which saw such things as literal and shameful. Western deities frequently marry, fornicate or breed brother to sister—Zeus and Hera, Demeter and Poseidon, Cronos and Rhea, even the Egyptian Isis and Osiris. (While it is not ancient per se, this incest is also echoed in Wagner's *Die Walkure*, where Siegmund and Sieglinde fall in love and breed the hero Siegfried.) In most of these cases (the Egyptian nobility being an anomalous example), it is very much understood by the mortal worshipers that this kind of incest was not for mortals, and would result in disaster if this divine privilege was stolen. Only the Gods could carry off such behavior ... and, really, in creation myths where there are only a handful of children born of a creator deity, who are they to marry except for each other? At any rate, it seems that Frey and Freyja may well have been invoked as a sexual sister-brother pair for purposes of divine fertility.

Another interesting correlation between the Divine Twins is that they are both associated with boars. While modern Heathens tend to concentrate on Freyja's "cat totem", she has a magical boar—Hildesvini—that matches Gullinbursti, her brother's steed. In the saga *Hyndluljóð*, Freyja turns her protégé Ottar into a boar in order to sneak him past Hyndla. Beyond this, on Yule Even the greatest boar was sacrificed to Frey as the *sonargoltr*, the "atonement boar", to persuade the god to grant a good year, and it is on the head and bristles of this sacred animal that King Heidrek (in *Heidrek's Saga*) and his followers placed their hands and took their most solemn oaths.[5]

The boar is one of the few animals that is reflected in both a wild and a domestic (pig) form; the two are not that far apart genetically, and feral pigs tend to back-breed to boars fairly quickly. The boar/pig is a liminal figure; as a wild creature it is hunted for food and can be tamed to become domestic food, but it always retains its wildness. It is the only domestic food creature that has been known to eat its young. It is associated in many cultures with death goddesses because of this, but not the sort of "deathrealm" goddess that Hel might be. Rather, swine were the provenance of the devouring Earth Mother (Demeter among the Greeks, Cerridwen among the Celts); their colours of white, red and black, their lunar horns, and their fertility (bearing litters of up to ten piglets) show them to be her children. Thus, the pig brings the Twins back to their Mother, Nerthus. One wonders if there is an echo here, with this sacrifice-devouring mother, of the fact that

---

[5] Chaney, William. *The Cult of Kingship in Anglo-Saxon England.* Manchester University Press, Manchester, UK. 1970

pig flesh has a taste and consistency very like human flesh, due to their omnivorous diet and muscle-to-fat ratio. The pig is the almost-human, between tame and wild, the replacement sacrifice.

All research aside, how do I see the Frey/Freyja relationship at the end of the day? As a Freyjaswoman, I know that she has the kind of almost-telepathic deep merging with her brother that many twins have, or are rumored to have. They know when the other is hurting and instinctively reach out, even as they live generally separate lives. I believe that when Frey is in Asgard, away from his wife, Freyja is his solace and gives him special comfort at that time. I also see Frey as being Freyja's anchor in many ways, as she is the more chameleonic of the two. When she is overwhelmed by woe—when she weeps tears of amber—it is often to Frey, the more "settled" twin, that she turns.

They love each other with a love that ranges from childlike and innocent to sexual, yet there is no possessiveness in it. After all, they are both Gods of love, and there is always more than enough love to go around between them. In a way, their relationship is a beautiful example of a loving and sometimes sexual relationship where the participants do not need to be married, or even partnered with each other romantically, for they look elsewhere for those needs. They are not each other's mate, they are each other's other half, which is a different situation. To learn about one is to learn about, and love, the other.

Solstice Morning
Elizabeth Vongvisith

Sunrise
and the stones are wet with dew,
shining erect in circles, surrounded
by grass growing lush and green.

Sunrise
and a bird's call wakens the people
from their soft summer sleep,
brings them blinking and joyous
into the radiance of this longest day.

He stands, stretches, muscle and bone
taut under tawny skin, hair flowing
in a cascade of gold, smiling, teeth
white and lips waiting to catch
the breath that bursts through.

Under a different roof,
her hands draw a comb
through her matching tresses falling
in glowing showers over her shoulders
and rounded, soft breasts.

Morning
and the day widens, bluer than blue
as the dancing commences with singing
under the green boughs, laughter
echoing in the fields and forests
while women and men chase and catch
each other, folding arms and bright eyes,
the sweetest honey of kisses, the fertile
scent of earth spreading herself to the sky.

Morning
and they dress, each
in robes of brilliant white, shining glorious
in the cool shadows of their separate dwellings
as their attendants make merry with fruit,
flowers, mead and water as clear
as the eyes that gaze knowingly
across the gentle green fields to where
he has come out of his magnificent hall,
waiting for her, his twin.

The procession arrays itself in splendor
born of plenty, of surety and abundance:
gossamer robes, feathers and the softest,
thinnest deerskin, sparkling stones, leaves
and flowers crowning heads, bright ribbons
and banners and above them, the solar wheel
fixed in gold, shimmering, a pale twin
of Sunna's radiant chariot racing above.
But below her turning wheels, neither
is the shadow of the other, both are golden,
magnificent, the power of life and love
walking in two forms that were once one,
and will soon be so again.

Trumpet blasts, the cry of excitement, birds
rising in calling flocks, the music and shouts
as the twins are escorted across the fields,
barefoot, flowers springing lush and fragrant
beneath their feet, born of every step, hands
intertwined, hair blowing in dual flags of spun gold
in the warm summer wind, robes pressing
and draping over bodies formed so perfectly
by the hand of some unseen master,
and now it is time.

Noon
and the shining pair walk alone
into the center of the largest circle, pillars
of stone thrust into the softness of earth,
grass tickling their feet, flowers arising
from every fated step, while the procession
circles around, singing and dancing, throwing
grain and gold into the circle, showering
the life of the fields and the life of the earth
with more and more and yet more.

Now she smiles, turns those cornflower eyes
to her brother, touches his face, the old magic
swirling around them as his eyes slip shut,
his hands search and find her, his mouth
closes over his twin's, this magic made today
as it has for thousands of years, and they fall
like the rain of an August afternoon
to bless and replenish the earth,
together as they once were in
the dark, secret womb of their mother.

Her sweet sigh shatters the stillness within
the circle as he rises into her; his laughter
breaks the rippling air into mirages.
Flesh moves on flesh, flowers and grasses wave
around their twining bodies, the deepening echo
of the oldest magic there is.

The dancers whirl madly, their song rising
to a pinnacle of feverish delight, her voice
and his climbing to reach and surmount
that beckoning place, and at last the earth ripples
under the interlinked bodies, the dancing feet,
the stones and the trees, the power rising

in a wave of passion and love to bless all
within the great pulse of magic and begin
the tumble of the year into darkness.

Noon
and the land renews itself
from the love of its lady and lord,
the exuberant songs and dances of its people,
the bright flowers whose soft petals splash the land
with color until they wither and fall, blown away
by an unseen wind faintly tinged with cold.

Litha Rite for Frey: High Summer

Gudrun of Mimirsbrunnr

This ritual can be adapted for a solitary worshiper, a couple, or a group. When I perform this ritual, I use a horn and a necklace of large chunks of amber, and a bottle of mead. Stand outside in full sunlight and place the items on a cloth of green and gold. Pour the mead into the horn and speak the following invocation:

Vanaguð, ágetasti af asum, folkum stýrir,
We hail you, mighty Frey and wise,
The green that we greedily devour,
The gift to our craving bellies.
You are the gift of high summer,
Green as the grass we lie in,
Golden as the light on the leaves.

Hold up the string of amber so that you can see the sunlight through it, and speak the following invocation:

Vanadis, fegjafa, fagr-ferðugr,
We hail you, fair Freyja and wise,
The blossom that yields to fruit,
The fruit that bursts in our mouths.
You are the gift of high summer,
Green as the grass we lie in,
Golden as the light on the leaves.

Sprinkle a bit of the mead in all directions, and speak this invocation:

Hail to the Vaettir of the land
That cradles my footsteps and traces my path.
I come to ask for blessings, for wealth
Of growth, of light, of all things come to fruition.

Pour out the mead onto the grass, and speak the following invocation:

Bless this land, O Sacred Twins,
Brother, sister, children of Earth,
Givers of fertility of tree and flower,
Of animal and human, of all life.
As I offer you the honey's kiss
I see you, Golden God and Goddess,
Double blessing sprung from one womb
One fair day in great Vana-land,
Come together as one light, one sun
Brought down to earth and earthly power!
Gift this land with blessed growth,
May blossoms rush to luscious fruit,
May leaves and stems grow lush and tall,
May seeds hang ripe in clusters heavy,
May roots swell beneath the turned earth.
May no disease or blight find us
In our safe harbor of earthen goodness.
Come together, Sacred Twins,
Tvifaldleikr, Gullbjartr,
Entwine your bodies and your hearts
With all the holy land around.

As these words are spoken, twine the string of amber about the horn, which is now empty and point-upward. When it is tightly twined, set the horn down where you have poured out the mead, bow to the horn and amber, close your eyes in respect, and back away. Let the energy of the Sacred Twins work through what you have left in the grass. At the end of the day, when the rays of the sun are dying away, come and retrieve the horn and amber and separate them, and silently thank Brother and Sister together.

Litha Recipes for a Frey Feast

Roast Suckling Pig
Seawalker

For this, all you need is a killed and prepared suckling pig, if you can get one from the local pig farmer or butcher, and salt, butter, and whatever herbs you like on pork. Rub the carcass with salt inside and out, place it on a rack that sits on a pan to catch the drippings, and roast it for an hour and a half at around 400 degrees. After the first half hour, check it every ten minutes. Wipe off the beads of moisture that will appear on the pig skin, brush it with melted butter, and add a little cold water to the drippings so that they don't burn and smoke. Keep doing this every ten minutes until it's done.

Fruit and Nut Dumplings
Seawalker

Ingredients:
8 medium baking potatoes
1 ¼ cups flour
2 beaten eggs
½ tsp. ground nutmeg
½ cup sliced and halved almonds
½ cup chopped walnuts
8 European plums, pitted
16 cherries, pitted
1 cup breadcrumbs
5 tbsp. butter
Powdered sugar

Cook potatoes in water until tender, cover and refrigerate overnight. Then mash them up with the flour, beaten eggs, and nutmeg to form a firm paste. If it's still too moist, add more flour. Place a half almond inside each of the cherries, and a bunch of walnut bits inside each of the plums. Roll dumpling dough around each fruit, smoothly enclosing it. The plums make big ones and the cherries make small ones. Bring a large pot of salted water to a boil and add the dumplings. Immediately reduce the heat and simmer for 20 minutes. While they cook, melt the butter in a skillet and sauté the breadcrumbs until golden brown. Take out the dumplings, roll in breadcrumbs, sprinkle with powdered sugar, and arrange on a platter with the plum ones in the middle and the cherry ones around the outside.

Stuffed Eggs with Sorrel
Seawalker

Ingredients:
8 eggs
3 tbsp. sour cream
3 cups chopped sorrel, picked fresh
2 tbsp. butter
Pinch salt
3 tbsp. cream

Hardboil 6 out of 8 eggs and shell, carefully. Don't cook the eggs too long or the yolks will discolor. Beat the other 2 eggs. Slice the boiled eggs carefully in half lengthwise and remove the yolks; mash them up and mix them with the beaten egg and sour cream. Wash the sorrel and pat dry, then sauté briefly in the butter along with the salt. Let it cool, then chop it fine. Mix the sorrel and the butter into the egg yolk mixture and use it to fill the egg white halves. There should be some left over. Butter a shallow baking dish and pack the stuffed eggs into it, filled side down. Stir the cream and another pinch of salt into the remaining mixture, pour it over the eggs, and bake at 300 degrees for about 15 minutes.

Golden One

Prayer to the Corn King
Ari

We sing to John Barleycorn, golden and tall,
We sing for the beer that we pass in the hall,
We sing for the bread that we break with our folk,
We sing for the bull beneath knife's silver yoke.
We sing for the harvest before it arrives,
We sing for the blood that is spilled for our lives.

We mourn for the grain that falls proud to the ground,
We mourn for each stalk of sun that we cut down,
We mourn for each root we tear up from the soil,
We mourn for each backbreaking hour of toil,
We mourn for each wish that will never come true,
And we mourn, truth be told, because some of them do.

Hail to Ingvi who dies that we might live,
Hail to each life that the great Nerthus gives.
Hail Ingvi the Corn King, golden and tall,
Hail to your rise and your glorious fall.

Golden One

Raven Kaldera

This song was written for Frey as a Lammas piece for the Asphodel Choir—
or perhaps it is more that Frey dictated it, and it was written down.

First Chorus, in two parts, slowly (♩ = 66):

First verse, all together, more quickly (♩ = 88):

Second Chorus, same tempo as verse. Second Verse, all together:

Third Chorus, slowly (♩ = 66).
Fourth Chorus, softer and wordless. First part "ooh", second part "ah".

Frey's Road
Jack Roe

The laughing lord leaves the locks
Of Woden's world, and wends his way
Through seas of thirsty salt, the sands
Of Vana land lie long and veiled leagues
From where fair Frey fares forth.
His father's ship fears not the shoals
Of Vana shores, its well-hewn walls
The waves repel, the rippling weed
Of mermaid's manes delay him not.
The dearest lord dismounts in time,
In summer's silken season. The singing
People pour out their welcome.
Waes hael the Golden God, who gives us
All. The elm and alder, apple and poplar
Watch his progress among the people,
Watch the women who throw themselves
At Frey's feet, their bodies to be blessed
By his fine phallus. He rides the road to
The final field, his horse's hooves
A booming beat that binds his doom
As his hands are bound by daisy chains.
Crowned and wreathed, he rides ahead.
The waving wheat, the woman waits,
Her sickle sharp as summer rains,
Her visage veiled in raven's raiment.
He kneels, he knows the need, he smiles
And lifts his living throat to this, the end
That is not an end. The blade, the beating
Heart and blood that seeps scarlet
Into the earth. The howl goes high,
The hue and cry, the wailers wander
Far and wide, the word to spread,

The blood's been shed, the babes will live
And bellies filled, and filled again.
We do not see the winding road
He walks each year, to Hel's hallowed home
Where softly sleep the sighing dead,
The dread and darkling gate that grows
From snow and ice. The maiden Mordgud
Merely smiles, her spear cast aside,
She greets the golden one with kisses
Caught only once a year. You have come,
And now you must go. Doom's door does not
Open for you yet. Next year, then, this time?
And so he turns, but only two steps takes
Before his vision blurs, the veil between
The worlds is whirled, his head is held
On the lap of love. Gerd washes away
The gash, the hurt, her gift of kisses
Life's instead of death's, and it is done.
The folk fed, father, mother, daughter, son,
And this is why he is the Golden One.

Lammastide
Elizabeth Vongvisith

I can remember, son of my womb,
when you were born, nudging your way
gently from between my parted thighs to rest,
gasping and mewling, on my breast
while your sister came out laughing.

You and she, the most precious of any gifts,
and I, the dark priestess, the Veiled One
forever cast into shadow next to
your ever-shining, twin golden flames.
It is there I will wait for you, unseen,
to return from that land of greater shadow.

The procession moves slow and solemn down
a well-worn dirt track between fields bursting
with rye and barley, between row upon row
of plump and shining fruits hanging from limbs
as graceful as your sister's slow walk.

She holds your hand easily, freely, only
a tiny line between her pale brows giving away
the feelings that will not rest, no matter
how often she must witness this,
the terrible beauty of sacrifice.

And the other, paler still, dark hair braided
like a crown for a queen without a realm—
she clings to your arm, her expression still
as the soft snows of winter on the ground.
Her tears will not fall until you do.

We come to the place, a hollowed stone

lying on its side, placed there so long ago
few now remember whose hands laid it.
I do, and I recall the faces of those long dead.
It seems fitting, given what I must do.

You embrace your twin, her shining hair falling
like a curtain around you both, then she steps
back among the assembly, her lips smiling,
her eyes hard and steely as a naked blade.
Your wife lays her head on your shoulder.

I see your eyes, blue as the deep sky, earnest
and knowing, gaze out past her shoulder
to the ripening fields and the fecund gardens
and now it is your lips that smile, your hands
that soothe as you kiss her and gently part.

The sickle is heavy and cold in my hand.
I gesture to the stone, where others come forth
and lay down armfuls of grain, loaves,
casks of beer, the first fruits of the year,
and step back, bowing, waiting for the moment.

Someone begins a low hum which swells
into a chant, the rhythm keeping time
with the beating of your heart which only I,
your mother, can hear as I raise the blade
like a sliver of molten silver in the sunlight.

O golden king, journey hard and fast
to the silent lands for this night
and return to us on the morrow.
O golden king, your blood waters
and makes fruitful the ground, rise,
rise reborn from the fields fallow

O golden king, Death is waiting
with arms outstretched, go to her,
go and return to us on the morrow.

And you smile, so that only I can see.

A language no mortal man yet remembers
thrumming like the song of insects from
the trees surrounding our fields, and now I move
faster than lightning to open your throat.
I step back and watch your light dim and go out.

Blood spatters the harvest, sprayed across
the stone, pooling in your white robes,
making long crimson rivulets across the dark,
moist soil as your body topples, golden hair
full of blood, your mouth open around silence.

Your bride's tears fall like another rain of blood.
Your sister opens her eyes and steps forth,
putting a slender arm around her, leading her
from this place, and the crowd parts as it does
every year, people falling into line behind.

I stand still, blood dripping from the sickle.
The procession retreats, mourning cries and wails
of sorrow high on the warm summer air.
I alone will stand watch until you return
from Hela's kingdom, and I alone will see:

first the hills forming the features of your face,
all this streaming golden grain becoming your hair,
every river leaping, shining, fish-filled and bright
with the gleam in your eyes, the flat fertile plains
becoming taut muscles of your body, trees strong

forming the pillars of your bones, and your cock
bursting with life and showering these lands
with the snowfall of winter and flood of spring
to make them yield and nurture and put forth
all that our people need to survive and thrive.

I will see you echoed in this land when Sunna
comes rioting over the edge of the world, her
long hair blazing, laughter echoing as the ground
erupts, splits apart and sprouts, turning green,
greener, then golden, barley lifting its head
towards the sun's skirts, birdsong triumphant,
and the pulse of your blood singing in every cell
of every plant and beast and being, your return
warming even myself, wrapped in the darkness
of under-earth and night and deep bogs,
you, my son, the sacrifice that gives and gives
and gives me a smile as you rise whole and stand,
alive again, alive, so that I can at last revel
in the bittersweet joy of what we have done,
in the gladness and glory of another year gone.

Frey's Lesson: Sacrifice
Raven Kaldera

This was first published in my two-book series *Wyrdwalkers* and *Wightridden*, but I really felt that it should be shared here as well. It was the most important thing that Frey ever taught me. I am a shaman and a god-slave, and I live a very narrow and focused life because of that. It often feels like something between a priest and a monk. I asked Frey for help in bearing this life, and this is what he taught me.

Frey is tall and golden and beautiful, and when he smiles it's like the Sun coming out. I met him the first time that I traveled in Vanaheim, and I fell in love. My relationship to him is very different from that of my patron deity. I work for her. I don't work for him, except to horse him once a year, and that's a separate deal that I made for him in return for a favor I asked. I've occasionally wished that I could be a Freysman, but I'm well aware that my nature is too dark and twisted for anyone but Her Ladyship to keep in line. Besides, the fact that I don't work for him means that I am free to just love him, and that's excellent in its own way. I don't think I really experienced the path of pure devotion until I met Frey.

It was a surprise to me when he required me to lend my body for one day a year in return for the favor he did me—not because I didn't think he could possess me, but because I was surprised that he would want to. I'm not tall and young and gorgeous, with the world's most beautiful cock, but that didn't matter to him. Besides love, I asked, where is the affinity? He is a creature of light and fertility, I'm a thing of darkness and sterility, a "black shaman" in Siberian terms (which doesn't mean evil, it just means that you work primarily with underworld deities). He reminded me gently that if he hadn't loved darkness as well, he would never have fallen in love with an etin-woman. "I am the light of Love that descends to the darkness," he said, "as my sister is the light of Love that seeks upward flight."

Affinity? There, too, he had an answer. "You are a sacrifice," he said, "just as I am, although in a different way. All the wight-workers who are chosen and bound, you are all sacrifices. And those who bind you are in haste, and they may not get around to teaching you how to properly be a sacrifice before you are thrown into it, if indeed it occurs to them at all." And it became clear that this was the lesson Frey had for spirit-workers, the thing that he felt they needed to know more than anything else. This is what he told me:

There are three parts to being a proper sacrifice. First, suffering. Second, usefulness. Third, joy.

The first one, suffering, that is the one that catches everyone up. One may sacrifice one's self for a cause, a loved one, for the greater good—but that is different. You are your own to give away, and if you have any sense you do not do that unless the cause is great, and if you waste yourself on a foolish cause you will eat the dust from that and learn better next time. But you do not know what a great and terrible thing it is when the Gods choose someone to sacrifice. We may not do this out of whim—I cannot stress that enough. There must be what your Ladyship calls Dire Necessity, the knowledge that without aid all will fail. In order to sacrifice the needs of one for the needs of all, there must be a great and terrible reason. The Norns guard those threads fiercely, and any God who would seize someone away from their life path without their leave must justify it to Urd's old, old ears.

The suffering that you go through, the remolding, the changing, the binding, this gives you great maegen. You cannot gain that kind of maegen on your own; it must be earned through outside circumstance, through some kind of struggle. When the knife comes through me, every year at the harvest, I feel that pain. It is never any easier. Do not think I do not understand your pain, you who have died and returned. Imagine having to do that every year. Imagine seeing the wheat-heads ripening on the stalks and thinking, Soon I will be dead. Over and over. That is the way of things. Something must die that others may live, eh?

You know that. You are that. I am that. It is what we have between us, you and I.

Then, after the suffering—the part that you people obsess on so—there is the usefulness. And this is where the maegen unfolds. If it was dire necessity that took you, you will gain much power by being useful in the way that alleviates it. For me, the corn must be cut, the grain must come down, the calf must be led to slaughter, or the people will starve. To come back and see them with full bellies, it is enough. It is always enough, and more than enough. Everyone you aid is the reason for your sacrifice. When you ask, "Why?", look at them. It is not enough to suffer. Your thread will not be made clean by mere suffering; that is only the first part. After you have endured suffering, you must alleviate it in others.

Everything you are will be used. You can sing—good. Then you will sing spirit songs. You have rhythm—good. Then you will drum for the spirits. You are quick of finger—good. Then you will spin spells. When you are a sacrifice, you retain nothing of yourself, and in exchange you gain.... what? Work. Work so worthy that the Gods obtained leave to sacrifice you for it. Can most people say this of their lives?

Your sexuality too, that will be used as well. Whatever is between your legs will no longer be your own, and that goes for those who do not carry Gods in their bodies as well. It is a tool, a great tool, a magnificent tool ... and it must be used that way. The man who places his member in the earth to give her a gift, or in his wife to give her children, that is a sacrifice in its own way. Yet many wight-workers must give up their fertility, aye, and that is why there is a second path in my sight .... the ergi ones with the bells on their skirts. Do you know how much maegen there is in sacrificing part of one's manhood, or perhaps all? Of course you do. And this, too, is given up. It is not yours. It belongs to the world now, and to the one who shapes your path.

And then, after the usefulness, the joy. This is the one thing that is not for them, and if you can achieve it you should try. First, because if you cannot learn to take joy in it, the Work will eat you quicker than it would otherwise. The joy is your buffer against the grinding, the honing, the hard use you are put to. It will give you that extra spark when the cycle comes around again and it is the dark time. Second— and this I tell you true, trust me on this—there are laws about what the Gods can and cannot use. Your body, your sex, your mind, your powers, your emotions, your eyes, your mouth, your hands—all these things they can use, if you are a sacrifice. But if you can find joy in it somehow, they cannot use that. It is against the Rules. It works for no one but you. And if you should want to have one thing that is still yours alone, it will be this ... if you can find it.

That is the secret ... if you can go to the pain and the sacrifice like the bridegroom going to his bridal bed, that can never be taken from you, or used to fuel the ends of others, even if those ends are great and worthy, even if it would save lives. That joy is yours to do with as you will, hoard it or give it, lend it or throw it away, and even the Norns themselves will not begrudge whatever you might choose to do. For this you have earned, by losing the rest of yourself, and by giving that to the world, and then struggling further to find this light. What is thrice- earned in this way is your gold. Follow it. It will be the only thing that you can be sure of holding onto.

Lammas Ritual for Frey: John Barleycorn
Raven Kaldera

Lammas is the biggest of the Frey rites, as it celebrates his death and rebirth as the Sacrificial King. It is a large public rite, with many parts. A fine altar should be laid, draped in gold and bearing many sheaves of grain bound with fine ribbons, corn dollies, symbols of Frey including small boars, little folded-paper ships, beehives, small figures of livestock, baskets of produce, carved phalluses, bundles of hops, etc. A bottle of red beer (it can be dyed with beet juice) and a horn of ordinary homebrewed ale sit there as well. A large fancy loaf of bread is also laid out; we suggest the Lammas wheatsheaf bread recipe at the end of this chapter. A large black cloth is folded and placed to one side. Nearby, a great feast is spread for everyone to eat.

A Frey figure is made, large enough to be seen by the crowd, and it is placed with flowers, grain sheaves, ribbons, etc. in a "wain" or wagon. This can be a large basket carried like a sedan chair by volunteers (perhaps wearing the horns of livestock animals) or a good-sized wagon, painted with appropriate runes. The wagon is pulled in procession with all participants singing the folk song "John Barleycorn". Each participant is given a handful of grain and they are encouraged to toss bits of it at the Frey figure, at each other, at passersby.

Four people stand at the four directions, two in each direction and recite the stanza from the Anglo-Saxon Rune Poem in Old English, and then the modern translation. In the north, the person holding a cow's horn speaks:

Feoh byþ frofur fira gehwylcum;
Sceal ðeah manna gehwylc miclun hyt dælan
Gif he wile for drihtne domes hleotan.

Wealth is a comfort to all men;
Yet must every man bestow it freely,
If he wishes to gain honor in the sight of the Lord.

In the east, the person holding a sickle speaks:

Gyfu gumena byþ gleng and herenys,
Wraþu and wyrþscype and wræcna gehwam
Ar and ætwist, ðe byþ oþra leas.

Generosity brings credit and honour,
Which support one's dignity;
It furnishes help and subsistence
To all broken men who are devoid of aught else.

In the south, the person holding a stag's antler speaks:

Ger byþ gumena hiht, ðonne God læteþ,
Halig heofones cyning, hrusan syllan
Beorhte bleda beornum ond ðearfum.

Summer is a joy to men, when God, the holy King,
Suffers the earth to bring forth shining fruits
For rich and poor alike.

In the west, the person holding a sheaf of grain speaks:

Ing wæs ærest mid East-Denum
Gesewen secgun, oþ he siððan est
Ofer wæg gewat; wæn æfter ran;
Þus Heardingas ðone hæle nemdun.

Ing was first seen by men among the East-Danes,
Till, followed by his chariot,
He departed eastwards over the waves.
So the hardy ones named the hero.

The main officiant steps forward and calls out: "Til ár ok frið!"
All shout it back. Then the officiant speaks the Invocation to Frey
found elsewhere in this book, then says:

> On this day we stand forth to witness the sacrifice
> Of our beloved golden god, who gives himself
> To feed the fields with his blood.
> The magic of his blood, given back to the Earth,
> Makes it blossom forth in the spring,
> Makes it yield fully in the summer,
> Lets us harvest in the autumn
> That we may have enough through every winter.
> Without that which gives back to the Earth
> There is no giving forth.
> So we praise Frey's courage, and his great gift,
> And we pray to have such courage ourselves,
> And such perfect faith, when the need is upon us.

The second officiant steps forth, robed and veiled in black and
carrying a sickle. (This can also be the individual who called the east
quarter.) Ideally this should be a woman, but regardless of gender the
face should be hidden. The second officiant calls out:

> What will you sacrifice?
> What will you give up to live?
> What will you give up that others might live?
> What will you give to Ingvi, for his sacrifice?

She goes from one to another, holding the sickle next to their necks,
each in turn. The people tell her what they are willing to sacrifice for
the year.

To complete the rite, the first officiant holds the longest
bunch of grain up, and the second officiant cuts it with the sickle.
The stalks are allowed to fall to the ground, and the sickle is held

over them, and the red beer is poured over it. The beer hallows the sickle and spatters like blood on the fallen grain. The first officiant goes to the wagon and reverently takes out the Frey figure, and lays it on the grain. (If there is concern about protecting it from beer-spills, a cloth may be laid down first.) The large black cloth is then spread over the figure, and the officiants both cry out, "It is done!" The people wail and cry out, and a group of well-rehearsed singers sing the song *Golden One*, found in this chapter.

Then the first officiant brings the harvest bread over and says, "Eat of His body, and live, and believe that He will live again." The people tear pieces from the harvest loaf until it is gone, and eat them. One piece is placed on the black cloth, and another back on the altar. The officiant passes the cup of beer and says, "Drink of Him, and be grateful, and be blessed." Then the officiant goes to the feast table and sprinkles the last drops of the beer on it, saying, "We bless this food in the name of Frey, the Golden Lord of the Harvest, and may we never forget his sacrifice."

Afterwards, the great feast is eaten. A vigil is kept for the next three days over the shrouded Frey figure, perhaps by alternating people who are especially dedicated to Frey. Those who keep vigil are marked with the Inguz rune while they keep vigil, and are brought food and drink by people in the community. Various of the poems and songs in this book can be spoken and sung, when more than one are waiting together. At daybreak on the final day, the black cloth is removed and the Frey figure is carried back to its home. (If this rite is done outside and it threatens to rain, a canopy may be erected, or the figure and the beer-damp wheat can be scooped up in the shroud, without uncovering them, and brought inside to finish the vigil. Alternately, the ritual can be performed on a litter which can be carried inside and put in a place of honor for the three days.) Another loaf of bread, with an Inguz marked on it, is saved for a small celebration by the vigillers (and anyone else who wishes to attend) when Frey arises at last.

Lammas Recipes for a Frey Feast

Lammas Bread for Frey
Raven Kaldera

This is a version of the traditional harvest wheatsheaf loaf. I saw it made at a particularly beautiful Lammas ritual by a Pagan group I visited and began to make it myself, with my own touches. Because it is a work of art that takes a lot of sculpting, I suggest that the baker make it a day ahead and refrigerate it, or have several people helping.

Ingredients:
12 ½ cups white bread flour
4 tbsp. salt
2 tbsp. melted lard or butter
¼ cup powdered milk
1 rounded tsp. yeast
1 5/8 pints warm water
3 beaten eggs, 1 set aside separately
1 tbsp. cardamom (optional)

You will also need small, cleanable scissors, as many as you have helpers, and a large tray. I generally bake the bread on a large plain tray on tinfoil and transfer it to a fancy tray afterwards.

These ingredients make a strong, tight dough that makes good sculpting material, so don't try to do it with a bread machine or electric mixer. It will break it. This is handmade bread. First combine all the ingredients except for the yeast, water, and eggs. Dissolve the yeast in the water, make a well in the flour mixture, and pour in the yeast water and 2 of the eggs. Knead the dough for around 10 minutes until it is smooth and pliable. It's better to knead this recipe too much than too little. Wrap the dough in a plastic bag and let it rise for about an hour. It won't rise much because of the low yeast content, but it should rise a little.

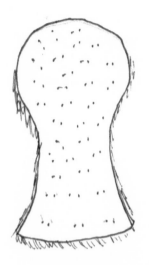

Roll flat a chunk of the dough. For the base of the wheatsheaf, you want a piece about half an inch thick, in the shape of a round bulb atop a wide flaring base. Generally my wheatsheaf is around 14" tall with the bulb around 10" across and the neck around 7" at its narrowest point. I form it directly on the tinfoiled tray where it will be baked. Prick it all over with a fork for ventilation.

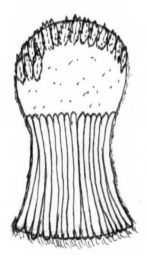

Then the fun begins. Everyone involved is going to roll long "snakes" out of the dough, the longer the better. They should be about the width of a pencil. Since the "stem" part of the wheatsheaf is 6-8" long, that's about what they should be. Keep a bowl of cold water handy and wet the dough base on the "stem" area as you lay on the "stems" to glue them on.

The upper bulbous part of the shape is the grain heads, which are also made from the "snakes". Take a "snake" and snip off about 2". Taking your small, sharp scissors, make a row of little "snips" at an angle up the side of the piece. Make a second row next to it, also angled upwards. Glue these down in rows with cold water, starting at the top and overlapping.

Take three long "snakes" and braid them together. Cut the braid in half and arrange it around the "waist" of the bread, knotting it. Leave the bread to rise another hour, with plastic carefully laid over it. Brush it with the rest of the beaten egg to give it a golden color. I like to arrange some nuts soaked for a few days in honey, for Frey, along the lower edge of the "grain" part. Bake at 400 degrees until it's perfect. Keep checking on it and turning it so that it will be browned evenly all over. Transfer it to a nice tray laid with a bed of greens and edible flowers (I usually tuck a couple of orange nasturtiums onto it) and serve for the Lammas feast, preferably with a bowl of honey butter to dip it in. (Mix equal parts melted butter and honey.)

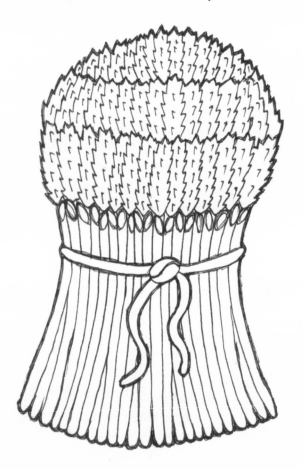

Cherry Bread Pudding
Seawalker

Ingredients:
2 pounds cherries, pitted (if canned, well drained)
10 or so slices of stale white bread
Butter
4 eggs
1 cup milk
¾ cup sugar
1 tsp. vanilla
Powdered sugar

Preheat oven to 400 degrees. Butter a deep baking dish and set aside. Spread each slice of bread with butter. Arrange the bread and cherries alternately in layers in the dish. topping with a bread layer. Beat the eggs until fluffy and beat in the milk, sugar, and vanilla. Pour the mixture over the bread and let sit for 5 minutes. Bake for 45 minutes or until the top layer has a golden crust. Sprinkle with powdered sugar.

Honey Ham
Seawalker

Ingredients:
1 10-pound ham or thereabouts
2 cups honey
4 juniper berries, crushed
1 tsp. fresh thyme
1 tsp fresh chopped lemon balm leaves
1 tbsp. salt
24 oz. dark craft beer
2 pears, chopped
2 apples, chopped
2 parsnips, chopped
2 carrots, chopped
2 golden beets, chopped

This dish marinates overnight, so start it the day before Lammas. The traditional way to prepare a ham is to cross-hatch the skin and fat on the top. When I make this dish, I take a sharp knife and carefully cut little Inguz runes all over the top—it works like a cross-hatch. Then put the ham in a large pot and smear it with the honey. Mix the salt and herbs and sprinkle them onto the honey layer. Pour almost all the beer in around it and let that marinate overnight. The next day, add the chopped fruit and vegetables around the outside of the ham, not covering its top, cover and cook the whole thing at 400 degrees until it is done. I put a knife down one of the Inguz cuts periodically to check. Add more beer over the top if it seems to be getting dry. Arrange the ham on a plate with the vegetables around it.

Marriage-God

Prayer for the Marriage-God
Ari

Hail to Frey, who fought for Love,
Who gave up gifts for etin-bride,
Who married across battle lines!
Hail Gerda, standing by his side!
Hail lovers, newlyweds, old hearts
That lean together like two trees
Entwined, enduring bonds so strong
That none denies what all can see.
Hail Frey and Gerda, Marriage-Gods
Who bless the unions few will bless,
Who stand by loves that bring up wrath,
Who sanctify each sweet caress
No matter what the others say.
Give us such faithfulness, we pray.

Invocation to Gerda

Raven Kaldera

Hail, Lady of the Walled Garden,
Hallowed in hedgerive and hammerwort,
Sacred in stonecrop and sowthistle,
Gifted and gifting in gladden and dragonwort,
You help us build the still, safe place
In which we can grow tender hopes to blossoming.

Hail, Lady of the forest paths,
Hallowed in hillwort and hindberry,
Sacred in cock's spur grass and sicklewort,
Gifted and gifting in gale and libcorn,
You help us bring those hopes into the world
To test and turn them into manifestation.

Hail, Lady of the quiet endings,
Hallowed in hulwort and whortleberry,
Sacred in ramsons and raven's leek,
Gifted and giving in viper's bugloss and boarfern,
You teach us to cull out what cannot be
While still keeping hope alive in the dark.

Hail, Lady of the hidden treasures,
Hallowed in mallow and meadowwort,
Sacred in sundcorn and stitchwort,
Gifted and giving in groundsel and sedge,
Cleansed in river-mint and lamb's cress,
You bring us deeper than we thought possible
Into the earth on which we depend.

Hail, Gerda, etin-bride of Frey,
Shadow to light, night to day,
All things balanced in your keen dark glance.

Garden

Raven Kaldera

Her eyes are like the shadows beneath the spreading mint,
Cool and dark, beneath that which reaches for the light,
But usually downturned upon her busy hands. It is never
That she is shy, merely that the calm darkness of her eyes
Full on is not a gift she shares often. Her gaze is the blessed shade
Of the honeysuckle tree when the sun beats down, unrelenting.
Woodruff spirals at its roots, at her feet, while the braver
Goosegrass bounds across the paving stones of my walled garden.

Her garden. After we put in the short post with her face,
Her wide-lipped mouth and averted gaze, it became hers.
No other northern goddess may have a shrine there, although
She thinks nothing of the clay Buddha and the painted Mariamne
Who were there before her. Gerda's peace lies on my garden,
Even now, when the green is November-withered and dull brown
Like the hems of her undergarments, brushing the stones
Around her ankles. All colors of the earth are kind to her.

Her hair is the color of rich earth, turned with a spade
Before the eager fingers, trembling with anticipation,
Push the seeds, gently, forcefully, into the soil. Its neat plaits
Are like the beds in early spring, when we turn back the straw
Mulch and see the quiescent brown, waiting for a touch,
As she waits patiently in her garden in Jotunheim
For the day when she will methodically make her way
To He whose touch is her yearly awakening. No other
Can rouse her sleeping response, can quicken her breath,
Can make her measured footsteps break into a heedless run.

We wanted the country, the farm, for many reasons, but truth
Be told, the thought of herb gardens made my breath catch
Longing in my throat. Fragrant lemon balm studded with bees,

Hoary sage, spiked motherwort and hyssop, and all the spilling
Mints. Yet I did not expect the bounty of the woods, when I
First walked this land—kinnikinnick, squaw vine, the scarlet
Berries of wintergreen against the December snow. As I built
The garden, bed by bed, my knowledge of the wild ones grew.
Wild and tame, they nourish me now. She loves all, though,
And so do I, as She has taught me.

Her back is broad, her shoulders like rolling hills, her arms
Strong with muscle. She is no delicate gilded thing; she walks
Among the elven people to meet her love, their gazes scandalized
And dwelling on the solidity of her Jotun form, her shape
A grandmother oak among their slender, ephemeral birch
And maple, hard like the oak and elm we split
To feed our kitchen stove, burning long and strong,
Not consumed for the hours it takes to bake
Those fragrant pies. Burning clean and bright, no black
Sludge in the stovepipe like those softer woods.
It is the hardest wood that lights the brightest fires,
A worthy match struck to His gold,
Passion to passion. Her patience is that woodpile, waiting sturdily
To light the coldest winter nights.

It took me seven years to clear the space. No tiller, no machines
In that rocky, half-sterile hill of patchy lawn, just me
And a garden claw hacking out the weedy turf piece by piece,
Square foot by foot, inch by aching inch. Patience, she said.
There is no deadline here. The magic is in the process,
Not the goal. One by one, the beds went in, stone edgings
Filled with compost dark as Her, rich from the manure piles
Of goat and sheep. One by one, the precious herbs.
If they did not survive, She said, Throw them out.
I want nothing here that is weak, that cannot
Stand up to wind and weather and perishing cold, here in this place
Whose winds and mountains are nothing to the bitter cold of my home.

Her garden is a spell of survival, of hope springing anew in spite of all.

Her touch is a stone wall, shutting out noise and bustle,
Protecting you from all that would overwhelm and frazzle you.
Her cheek is the paleness of thick roots that grow in the garden,
Buried and eagerly sought. Her body lies hidden beneath
Layers of dresses, plain and dark or brightly embroidered
By giantess-fingers—you would not think them nimble,
Compared to the elves who despise her, and yet her touch is soft,
Sure, and plies a needle well. Dark crescents of soil lie
Under her fingernails, from centuries of plying dirt as well,
On her knees in the gardens she loves, the tiny seedlings twining
Up to kiss those broad fingers, as they know how much
Love is there for them. Her love is the warmth of piled earth
In small mounds about their fragile roots,
Helping them to survive the frosts.

"It won't survive," I say mournfully, looking at the second black lamb
Whose tiny frame has lived these days only by our driving hands,
Pouring milk down its reluctant throat. Live, we say, like a spell
To give it will to do so, yet sometimes that spell fails. Mother-rejected,
It will not even mewl. That black ewe knows better, her baleful gaze
Protecting its stronger sister, who suckles happily. Sometimes they just
Know. Some life is meant to fail—that is the lesson of Life's profligacy.
Quantity first, then weed for quality. Time to Weed, Gerda says,
And we take the tiny body out in the cold, for the hammer-blow,
For the ceasing of that shallow breath, for the compost heap
That will turn death into more Life, come spring.

Her rare smile is sweet as elderberries, hanging in dark clusters
On the graceful branches, following the lacy white blossoms
That cure the cough and cold. Her womb is a barred gate;
No young will she bear her beloved, to be hostage to his keepers,
Though tears rack them both on many nights, together and alone,
When they speak of this pain. Her heart is a warm quilt,

Tucked silently over the sobs of the woman whose child
Did not come to fruition, or who had to stop
The child herself. Her tears are the cold rain that falls
On the lovers who cannot speak of something,
Whose words are caught and trapped, yet that rain
Will nourish the seedlings that fight their way upwards.

Because of the weeding, I spend more time kneeling before Gerda
Than any other. I pull, and kill, and kill. It is necessary, she says.
The beams of my kitchen hold bunches of herbs, to find their way
Into savory cooking, or into row upon row of shining glass bottles
For medicine. It was a hobby at first, a way to thwart the high cost
Of the pharmacy, a smug satisfaction … and then the people came,
Asking for help. The women were the hardest, the girls
With their wombs filled unwanted, fearing the machines
Of the doctors—was there not an easier way? I helped,
And sometimes we were lucky, and the clinic
Not needed. Do what is necessary, Gerda says. And I do.

Her soul is a deep cave under the earth, bored with holes
Like the sacred places under the ancient megaliths.
On sacred days, the sun shines through, and lights the
Bloodied stone table like a miracle. Pain and joy, and I kneel
To deeper wisdom. There must be culling, pruning, weeding
For there to be growth. His growth.
And this is her Mystery.

Hail the Golden God

Galina Krasskova

You are the joy-bringer of Asgard's halls,
A God of light and laughter, gentle pleasures
And a magnificent strength of such virility, such might
That well I understand how Your wife was first moved
By the sight of You,
Standing aching, hungry and heart-sore
In a sacred grove,
Strung between worlds
Beneath Mani's light.
Well I know how the two of You
Became each other's sanctuary,
Each enfolding the Other
In desire and liquid heat
Until the worlds fell away
And there was only the ecstasy
Of hands, lips, tongues and flame:
A serenade of ecstatic moans
Heralding the union of shadow and light
Beneath the gaze of the silent moon,
Who is good at keeping secrets
And will never tell
Of the sweetness
Of Your surrender.

The Hungry Golden God

Galina Krasskova

My hungry Golden God,
Delight of Gerda's body,
Ever hard, ever desirous
of Your fierce and mighty bride,
You come with the pulsing, pounding rhythms
of the seed fighting for light
through the resistant body
of the rich and sultry earth.
Mighty and proud,
You wooed and won
 The fiercest of Gymir's get.
You filled Her with light, as She enveloped You with darkness.
You are fierce in Your love, courageous, the bravest of warriors.
Would Gerda have accepted anything less?

Serving Gerda
Galina Krasskova

(Twice now, I have served Gerda by horsing Her at Lammas. "Horsing" is a term popularized in Afro-Caribbean traditions for the phenomena of Divine possession, the idea being that the God or Goddess "rides" the human much as a rider upon a horse. For lack of a better term, those of us within Heathenry and Norse Paganism who practice this also call it "horsing". Deity-possession is a process whereby a person's consciousness is moved aside and the God or Goddess inhabits the human's body, using it as He or She will. For those born with the appropriate psychic and mental wiring to allow this to occur, it is an amazingly intimate way to serve a God.)

Shrouded in stillness You come,
silent and self possessed.
Watching and ready,
You sink into me, filling my flesh,
forcing me back, until my senses are Yours...
Your power a quiet thing,
an animal leashed and reined
by iron will ... as I am leashed and reined.
You notice everything and yet
and yet
Your eyes and heart and hands
seek only Him.
Enticer of Frey, Beloved Bride of the Lord of the Land,
He who is Bringer of bounty to all barren places
You hunger and in Your hunger
You clarify the pathways of the heart.

Gerd Meets Frey

Michaela Macha

Gerd:
"To Barri, the wood which both we know,
you compelled me to come, now answer!
Are you the Van who would woo me with threats
and never take no as reply?

Nor bribe of gold nor gruesome curses
will win the heart of a woman.
Always the gods deal ill with us giants;
why should I wed you, Frey?"

Frey:
"To turn your heart, my last hope were runes,
but your magic is stronger than mine:
Enspelled by your beauty I've spent my days
since I saw you from Hlidskjalf's height.

Little I care if I live or die,
if I feel not your arms enfold me.
I will honor and love you; even my father
wedded one of your kind."

Gerd:
"Why should go from my glaciers and rocks,
my home in the mighty mountains?
What shall become of the wastelands I own,
if indeed I would follow you, Frey?"

Frey:
"With green I will cover the grey of your mountains,
make fertile the rock-strewn fields.
Grass will grow on the ground that was barren,
a beautiful garden for Gerd.

Your realm's pride will be praised by men,
they'll honor you even as a goddess.
If you would have it, my heart is yours—
I offer you all that I own."

Gerd:

"I did not believe you love me so well;
now I've seen your soul in your eyes.
You've thawed the ice of an etin-maid—
gladly will Gerd be your bride!"

Note: This poem is in the Old Norse alliterative meter Ljodhahattr (Song Meter). This poem is copyright Michaela Macha in the Common Domain and may be freely distributed provided it remains unchanged, including copyright notice and this License.

Gerda's Three Weddings

Raven Kaldera

When Gerda was only a young girl, just about to come to her womanhood—which comes early to etin-women—she went with her family to Vanaheim for the first time. Her father and mother had gone to Vanaheim before, as the Jotunfolk who dwelt near the coast often put their hands into the trading between Vanaheim and Jotunheim. Gerda had seen the wooden carts, heavily laden with casks and boxes of foodstuffs, come trundling over the rough roads carved by giant hands through the jagged mountains and immense trees. She had tasted the soft, fine grains, better than any grain that could be grown in her heavily forested world, and the good ale from Aegirheim brewed with Vanaheim barley, and the great cabbages like giant green flowers sprouting from the Vanaheim soil, more fertile than any other in the Nine Worlds.

But it was nothing like finally walking on that soil, to seeing another world. Vanaheim was the first world other than her own that she had seen, and they traveled across the sea to get there in a ship that made her clutch the bow and try hard to still her stomach. Her mother fed her honey brewed with spicy roots to ease her belly, but even so she remembered that first trip as little more than a misery. She envied her older brother Beli his easy, cheerful climbing about the deck, and his mocking of her cramped misery did little to help. When he tormented her for the final time, waving a half-rotted fish at her and jeering, she got up unsteadily on her feet and threw a heavy coil of rope at his head, which knocked him overboard. Then their father had to fish him out by grabbing the other end of the rope, and their mother slapped and scolded her, but Gymir was laughing. "Don't push our quiet little Gerda too far!" he roared proudly. "She may seem like a mushroom, but she has the soul of a tiger-cat under there!" But Gerda sulked and chewed on the end of her black braid of hair until the trip was over.

The first thing that she noticed about Vanaheim was how open the land was. "Where are all the trees?" she asked, used to the thick crowding forests of her home; here, the woods were short and small and further between, and much of the land was patterned like a great quilt in fields of golden wheat and barley and rye, the red of kale and the feathery green plumes of dill and fennel, the yellow of mustard-flowers and the blue of flax-blossoms. They stayed at Billing's great hall on the Jotunheim-facing coast, for he was the master of all trade between the two worlds, and much respected in both. And when the hot summer was at its peak, they went to watch the sacrifice of the Corn King.

It was the first time that she laid eyes upon Frey, the Golden Lord of Vanaheim. He came to his yearly duty, tall and golden and smiling. He rode down the dusty road on a great white horse, and the people called out, "Ing! Ing!" as he came. The small knot of watching Jotunfolk stood to the side, a small pool of silence in the cheering crowd, and Gerda stood in the center of it. She watched him dismount in the wheatfield, where all but the last sheaf was cut down. The sickle flashed in the hand of someone clad in ragged grey, and the sheaf was swiftly wrought into a wreath to place on Frey's golden hair.

Gerda's mother and father, and even her older brother, had seen this rite before, and they hardly flinched when the knife went in and the golden-haired god fell to the earth, his blood soaking into the stubble-clad field. There was a scramble to get the cup filled and passed around, so that as many as possible might drink. After all the cheering, it seemed as if there was dead silence in the air, as if every voice had died with the golden Vanir man. Gerda did not wish to break the silence, so she waited until they had started down the road to Billing's hall before she said, "That was a shame, to kill him. He was a fine-looking man."

Her brother burst into jeering laughter, and even her mother chuckled. "That was Frey, one of the Lords of Vanaheim," her father told her, "and he dies in that way every year. If the ritual is done properly, he will be back to life in a few days and walking about, good as new."

"Every year, father? But cannot another take his place sometimes?"

Her father shrugged and said that he did not claim to understand the way of the Vanir. "But this is what Frey was born to do, it is said. It is part of the secret of Vanir fertility. And now we should take our supper."

Gerda had one more question, but she did not ask it, because she did not think that either her father or her mother had the answer. So she tucked away into the box of unanswered questions in her head, which was a very full box because she was still quite young.

Many years later, when she was a grown woman and most of her questions had been answered, a messenger came to her father's hall in Jotunheim. Gerda had grown into a tall woman, pale-faced with long hair the color of the dark turned earth. She was still quiet, but even her brother had learned by then not to push her too far. Once he ruined a thing of hers and laughed at her when she demanded wergild, and she turned into a lean black leopard and leaped upon him, scratching his face with her claws. It took her father ten minutes and three different shapes to pull her off of him, and it took her mother a month to properly heal Beli's face. After that, Beli walked cautiously about his quiet sister, and did nothing to make her eyes flash red at him in the shadows.

Gymir's hall was surrounded by a wall of fire, that no enemies might enter, although of course it wavered and split aside when any member of his household approached it from the inside, or a friend approached it from the outside. Yet this stranger came rushing through the flames on a blood-red horse, and the horse seemed not to be touched by the flames. As the folk of Gymir's household piled outside, her brother came up beside her, his hand on his sword-hilt. "A rune-charmed horse," he said. "This man must be sent by someone of power."

Her father came up beside them. "Mayhap," he said, "but I am the lord here, and he must still do courtesy to me." And he called out to the man to speak his name, and his errand, or a hundred arrows would lodge themselves in his head.

Gerda did not know that Frey, the Golden One of Vanaheim, had climbed the steps to Odin's tower Valaskjalf, the throne in front of the great window that looked out upon nearly all things. He had gone there just weeks before in order to search for his sister Freya, who had long been missing, searching for her lost husband Odr. The great wolves at the foot of the stairs, Geri and Freki, growled at him but let him pass, for his errand was good, and indeed he saw his sister turning back toward Asgard and returning to her summer home.

But then, as he would tell her himself much later, the glass shifted and showed a hall in the middle of a ring of fire, in the snowy winter of Jotunheim. Frey blinked, for until this time nothing in Jotunheim had interested him much, but he did not look away. The door to the hall opened, and an etin-woman stepped out and looked up, and for a moment it was as if she had locked eyes with him.

She locked eyes with him for only a moment, but it was enough for him. Frey, the Golden One of Vanaheim, sat on Odin's throne like a statue, his heart seemingly stilled in his chest. All he could see was those dark eyes, and her frown of concentration. He watched the wintry sun glint off of her nearly-black hair in its tight, elaborate braids pulled sharply back from her pale face, saw her height and broad shoulders and ample figure and the way she held her head high. Nothing else existed for him to see in that moment. Then she called out to someone in a voice that he could not hear, and waved, and he realized that she had not seen him at all. Her glance had been for someone beyond the gaze of Odin's mirror. Then she stepped back into the hall and closed the door.

Frey could not move from the seat of the throne all day, though he knew that Odin would be wroth if he found him there. He sat with his breath harsh in his throat, waiting only for one more glimpse of the etin-woman. He got one, just as the Sun was sinking over Asgard and he knew that folk would come looking for him. Night had already fallen in Jotunheim, and she came outside with a basket over her arm, accompanied by two other etin-women. The other two laughed and talked gaily, but she only smiled with that same self-enclosed look about her. Frey studied every inch of her face, her profile, the movement of her hands as they helped brush back the snow from a small cellar and pull out roots to fill their baskets. He drank in the pale flash of her throat as she adjusted the mantle around her shoulders, the same dark-earth color as her hair. He watched her braids fall forward as she stooped, and his heart fluttered as they brushed against the snow near her knees. Then she went back into the hall with her maidens, and the door shut behind them, and though he sat for many more hours, all was dark within the great carved-tree hall and no one came forth.

Finally he left the tower, and wandered up and down the moonlit road as if in a trance. When dawn broke and Odin seemed to be busy elsewhere, he returned desperately to Valaskjalf in the hopes of seeing her again. Geri and Freki growled at him and would not let him pass, though he ordered them and pleaded with them, for they could sense his desperation and felt that his errand was not pure of heart. Weeping, he fled to his father's hall on the shores of Asgard, Noatun, the white curved building given to him by the Aesir for the time of his hostaging.

Njord saw his son's red-rimmed eyes and haunted glance, and brought him to sit before the fire at his fireplace, the mantel of which was the bow of a ship. "My son, what ails you?" he asked in concern.

"I have seen a maiden," said Frey, and then realized that he would have to tell of being in Valaskjalf. But this was his father, who would put him before the Aesir, and so he told of it. "You have been to Jotunheim with the traders, my father," he said. "Do you remember a hall, near the shore, carved from a single giant tree as the giants often do, and surrounded by a ring of fire? Do you remember a tall girl with hair the color of turned earth in braids to her knees, with eyes as dark as shadow, with skin pale as Niflheim snows?"

Njord was silent for a moment and then shook his head. "A hall in a ring of fire, yes, that is Gymir's place. He is an etin-lord of great power, my son, and if your heart is set on his daughter, I can think that it will only go ill for you. Forget her, my son. There are hundreds of women in Vanaheim who would willingly be your bride, or if you will not have your own kind, there are fair ones here in Asgard as well. But the etin-women are fierce, and I see that you would have to endure great loss for her."

Frey raised shadowed, sleepless eyes to his father's face. "And why should I, who go willingly to the blade every summer, fear loss? What is it that I must lose?"

Njord was silent again, and said, "Of all your possessions, what is most fine to you?"

The golden god's hand went to his sword. "This," he said. "For it was a gift from my mother and from you, and the last thing I received before coming here as a hostage."

"You may have to give it up," said Njord, "if you continue on this path."

Frey unbuckled his sword-belt without a pause and flung it on the floor. "Then I will give it up," he said. "It is only a sword. This is far greater."

Njord took up the sword from the floor, and placed it back in his son's hand. "When you took up this magical blade," he said, "you swore an oath that it would be the only sword that you would ever wield. If you give it up, you will have no sword again, ever, and you will be defenseless. Please, my son, think again."

Frey stared into his father's eyes for a long time, and then he spoke. "I cannot live without her," he said. Then he turned and rushed from Noatun, clutching the sword, and spent many hours pacing up and down the roads weeping. He would not speak to any who saw him, and they wondered, and were concerned, for the Golden One of Vanaheim was never seen in sorrow.

It throbbed in his head. Gymir's daughter. An etin-princess, child of a powerful lord. His friends had warned him about etin-women. They desired them, it was clear, but they also feared them—not as much as an Aesir might, but enough. One did not seduce an etin-woman; they came to you on their own terms or not at all, and one certainly did not try to take her unwilling, or you might find yourself beaten bloody or torn to bits. And indeed, there were hundreds of fair maidens of his own race who would gladly—and indeed already had—shared his bed and considered it an honor, and if this should not be enough, nearly any unmarried woman of the Aesir—and some who were married—would fall willingly to his charms. Why bother with a woman of the Jotnar, a barbarian who would scratch you as soon as look at you, and whose kin would likely do worse?

But Frey spent the rest of the week wandering up and down the road, as if he could not decide where to walk, as if it no longer mattered where his feet took him. His friends tried to distract him with the usual delights and comforts, but his eyes merely stared into the distance, seeing darker ones that locked with his. He did not speak, and hardly ate or drank; when he arrived in Asgard, he went straight to his room in his sister's house, and would not speak to anyone.

Over and over, he recalled what he had seen of her. He wondered why she wore a covering dress that reached from her neck to her ankles, instead of the tendency of most young etin-women to dress in furs and knives, showing off their tall, strong bodies. He wondered if it was modesty, or merely a strong sense of privacy; he wondered what it would be like to see that dress pooling around her ankles. He wondered what her voice sounded like, and how that pale skin would feel beneath the touch of his hand. As the Golden One of Vanaheim, he had lain with more women—and men—than he could easily recount, yet he somehow felt that if he could be with this woman, all the others would fade away by comparison.

He knew also that if he lay with her the one time, he would never wish to leave her... and that was not done. His own people would look askance at an etin-bride; the Aesir to whom he was pledged would be even more disapproving, and the Alfar even more than that. Etin-women were to lie with and then leave; one would then take a civilized wife who would follow you about respectably and faithfully keep your household and raise your children, including any that you happened to make with such side-trips. *You could lie with her, and then forget her,* he told himself, and then he laughed. *No, you will never forget her. And she deserves better than that.*

Getting up his courage, he sent a message to where Gymir held summer court on the coast of Vanaheim, but the message was refused at the gate, for Gymir did not want a Van courting his daughter. The messenger was turned away, and Gerda did not know. When the letter was delivered back into his hands unopened, Frey was plunged into a deep sorrow. He did not leave his rooms at Sessrumnir, and spent many hours lying on his bed and weeping. A cloud of grey seemed to engulf him, and his golden light was dimmed entirely.

Freya came back to Asgard at this time, and though many of the Aesir came to welcome her, with tears or heartening words, her brother was not among them. And she was downcast to see this, and asked about him, and was told that he had not come out of his room in many days. She asked in fear if he was ill, not wishing to lose yet another of her kin, but Loki said, "Ill, yes, with an illness that you know well, Lady of Love, and that only one thing can cure. He has lost his heart to some woman who will have him not, and he will not speak to any of us of it."

Freya came to him at once and cried out to see him red-eyed and tossing in his bed. "Who is this woman who has done this to you?" she cried. "Only tell me her name, my brother, and I shall place a bewitchment upon her so that she might fall helplessly in love with you, and then this will all be over!"

But Frey refused her gift. "I would win her on my own terms and hers, for if she loved me by the power of magic, I would always fear that it might fail, or that without it she would care nothing for me." And Freya wept and kissed his forehead, and though she nodded she did not speak, although it tore her heart to see her brother this way. But it was now her time to go back to Vanaheim for the winter, so she bade him to try and sleep, and left his side.

Finally Skirnir, a half-Alfar friend from his youth, the first who had befriended the lonely golden-haired youngster when he had first arrived in Asgard, stormed his room in Sessrumnir. "My friend, what has become of you!" he cried. "Whoever this maiden is, we will get her for you, unless she be wedded to another, and perhaps even then, for marriages have often been broken beneath the plow of a handsome god! Who is this woman, my friend? Tell me and we shall plan our attack!"

Frey hesitated, but the truth burned within him, and he yearned to tell someone. When Skirnir heard, he laughed uproariously, and said, "So the Golden One of the Vanir is in love with a barbarian etin-maiden! This is fun indeed! Do you actually intend to marry her, or do you merely mean to plow her furrow, Fertile One?"

"I would do both, if I might," Frey said, "and more than that still, but I cannot even speak to her. She is well guarded in her father's hall, and her father likes not my suit, and sends back my missives. If I go there myself next summer, I would be killed, and at any rate I cannot wait that long. I think that longing for her might kill me before then."

Skirnir shrugged. "I could go there," he said, "and I could take a message. No oath binds me here. Of course, I would be risking my life, but I think that I could get through Jotunheim and impress some barbarian lord and his daughter."

Frey drew in his breath. "Would you court her for me?" he asked. "Would you arrange a meeting? I will be forever in your debt."

"What would you give me," said Skirnir cannily, thinking of Frey's great wealth, "if I were to do this for you?"

"Anything," Frey replied. "My horse, my boar, my ship—what do you want?"

Skirnir's eyes fell to the magical sword at Frey's side. It had been forged by the Duergar for Nerthus of the Vanir to give as a gift to her son, and its hilt was wrought like golden wheat and its blade was inlaid with many runes. "Give me your sword," he said, "for I want something to use in my hand, to stay by my side."

Frey was silent at this, and his thoughts warred with one another. His father's words echoed in his ears, and he looked back and forth from Skirnir to the sword. Finally he said, "Ragnarok is far away, and may not ever come. This is now." And, he thought, if anyone had to hold his sword, at least it would be his friend Skirnir. He held out the sword to Skirnir and said, "Go to Jotunheim. Convince her for me."

And so it came to pass that Skirnir came bursting through Gymir's wall of fire, armed with Frey's magical sword and riding Frey's magical red horse, Blodighofi, who did not fear fire. He backed the horse to the door and made it kick with its hooves, striking loudly. "Do we let him in?" growled Beli to his father.

"He may be rude and a fool," said Gerda, "but by the rule of hospitality he is owed a drink. And aside from a mark on the door, by which you and your own friends have done worse, my brother, he has not attacked us." And she went calmly to the door and welcomed him.

Skirnir introduced himself and his errand, and when Gerda heard that missives had come and that she had not heard, she cast a disgruntled glance at her father. Skirnir opened his pouch and showed her the jewels and magical apples that Frey had given him, and promised her more if she might marry his master, Lord Frey the Golden One of Vanaheim.

As she stood staring at the gifts, Gerda's heart skipped a beat in her chest. She remembered the tall fair-haired man whose throat had been cut, and how fine she had thought him. Then she hardened herself. Why did such a man not come before her himself? Why did he send some minion to bribe her with gifts, as if she was a thrall to be purchased? "Take your gold and jewels to other maidens," she said. "The daughters of Jotunheim are not so easily bought."

Skirnir's face darkened, and he drew the sword from his belt and waved it around in the air. "Agree to marry Lord Frey or meet your doom!" he cried.

Gerda stood her ground. Behind Skirnir, two dozen etins had their blades half out of their sheaths, watching for the word from Gymir. She set her jaw and glared at him. "Threaten the daughters of men with your blade," she said, "but do not try to frighten a giant's daughter with such puny things."

Skirnir's face turned red with rage and he began to rant, cursing her with a long litany of deaths and disasters if she did not submit at once. She stared at him, wondering if he had gone mad. Then the sword flashed through the air, and accidentally struck a beam, and one of the lamps fell to the floor with a crash, and everyone ducked, cursing. "Shall I kill him now, Father?" hissed Beli, his eyes gleaming.

Gymir gritted his teeth visibly. "Not yet, my son. I have an idea." Then Gymir pulled his daughter aside and spoke to her where only her family could hear. "You are my child, and I will never force you to wed where you would not," he said, "but my business is often in Vanaheim, and a marriage to the Golden One might be advantageous. At least meet with him, speak to him, and if you find him hateful I shall shelter you from all harm."

"But this fool is in your hall now, my father!" she hissed. "What shall I do with him?"

"Pretend to be frightened," said her father, "and say that you will meet with his master. That will get him out of here before he sets the ceiling on fire and we must slay him for it."

Gerda sighed and shook her head, for she was not one for dissembling, but she awkwardly knelt before the ranting Skirnir and pleaded with him to stop, that she would meet Frey and discuss marriage with him. "Where?" Skirnir demanded.

She thought of asking to meet him in the Iron Wood, and bit her tongue, trying not to smile. Perhaps somewhere in Vanaheim was best, she thought. "In the Barri Woods," she said, remembering the thick stand of trees where she had played as a child while visiting the coast of the Vanir. That reminded her of the one time she had seen Frey, which had been his death. *Could I marry a man who dies by the knife every year?* she wondered. "In nine days," she added, giving herself time to think about it.

Gymir stood forth then. "We must discuss the bride-price," he said, and Gerda was reminded that her father was very much a merchant. Still, it might distract this raving messenger. "My daughter is no mere milkmaid, to be had for nothing," he said.

The sword wavered in the air, and dropped. Finding now no opposition to his demands, and faced with an etin-lord ready to haggle, he was no longer on sure territory. "What would you ask, my lord Gymir?"

"That sword," said Gerda, pointing to it. "If he wants me, he will give his sword to my family." It was one way to get it out of this lunatic's hands, she thought.

Skirnir looked dismayed. "But Lord Frey promised it to me for my service here—" he began, but Gymir cut him off.

"No, no, if he will have my greatest treasure, I will have his! Tell your lord that no other bride-price will do, and that if he wishes to bargain, his wedding will be much delayed," said Gymir. "And you may leave that sword here, in token of your good will."

Skirnir stared at the sword, and at Gymir, and perhaps it occurred to him that Frey was in such a state over Gerda that he would gladly give away the sword to this family of Jotnar rather than delay the wedding for weeks while they haggled over precious stones and bales of grain. "Very well," he said sourly, "I will leave it here, by your threshold. But none may touch it until she is delivered to their wedding night!" Then he stalked out of the hall and leaped onto the red horse to leave, and all the fists of Gymir's men relaxed on their sword hilts.

But Beli stood forth angrily and faced his father. "My father must value his daughters so little, that he would sell them so cheaply without a fight! Why did you not allow me to slay the rascal, and then we would have had the sword anyway!"

"With how many of my men dead?" Gymir pointed out. "And even if you did kill him, then we would have the Aesir and the Alfar down on us, and a war would begin. Now, I do not mind a war or two, but the spring shipments are ready to go across the water, and—"

"These are the words of a trader, not a warrior!" cried his son. "You have sold my sister for credit in Vanaheim!"

Gerda put a hand on his shoulder. "I but promised to meet him and speak of marriage," she said. "I can still reject him, or if it comes to marriage, I can divorce him if I like him not. I am sure that I can find ways to make him sorry that he fell in love with me." And she bared her sharp Jotun teeth, and Beli snorted and went to look for some ale.

When Skirnir thundered back over Bifrost, he found Frey waiting anxiously by the gatehouse, next to where Heimdall kept his watch. Frey ran up and seized his stirrup. "Tell me what happened," he said urgently. "Before you even get off my horse, tell me!"

Skirnir tossed him a grin. "She is yours," he said. "She will meet you in nine days in the Barri Woods to discuss the wedding with you."

Frey's face went from dark to light to dark again. "Nine days!" he moaned. "It will be nine days of agony. But at least she will see me!"

Skirnir dismounted and pulled him aside. "There is one problem," he said. "Her family asks for your sword. I told them that you had promised it to me, but they were adamant."

Frey rent his hair. "Then they must have it," he said finally. "I give you my horse, Skirnir, as a gift instead." Then he went to Odin, and flung himself on his knees, saying that there was a family matter in Vanaheim that he must see to, and giving his word that he would return as hostage in one turn of the Moon's path. Odin saw his reddened eyes, and though he did not guess at the cause, he released Frey to go home for one month.

She met him in the woods, in the darkness, so that she would not have to look into his eyes at first. He brought a torch, but she called down a gust of wind to blow it out. He saw her only as a tall figure in the shadows, waiting for him, and it seemed that he saw as well the flash of red eyes in the darkness, and the graceful shadow of a great cat. She stood alone, draped in her dark cloak the color of the turned earth, her hands clasped before her. "So you are the one who has gone to such trouble to woo me," she said. "My father likes not your messenger. Why did you not come yourself?"

"I was afraid, Lady," Frey replied, and his voice was soft.

"Afraid of my father? He might have spitted you on a pike, that is true," she said.

He shook his head. "I would walk through many pikes merely to speak to you. No, I was afraid that I would fall to my knees before you and beg you to marry me, and that would shame us all in front of your family. I could not trust myself, so I sent Skirnir."

She was silent for a while, a still figure in the darkness. "You would have done better to come yourself," she said finally.

"Skirnir says that your father asks my sword as a bride-price," he said.

Gerda lifted her head proudly. "I ask that price," she said, "in exchange for my pledge to you. It was no idea but mine. Am I not worth your finest possession?"

"If you will marry me, you will be my finest possession," replied Frey. "I will gladly give up my sword to you. I would give you anything I have. But I am bound by my hostage-vows to fight with the Aesir, and if Ragnarok comes, it may be used against me."

"Then we shall have to make sure that Ragnarok does not come," she returned. "But I warn you, I will not dwell in the lands of those who killed my kin."

Frey shook his head. "I cannot break my hostage-vows. My father and my sister and I swore them on terrible ancient powers. I must live in Asgard or Alfheim for two-thirds of the year, and only visit my home during the autumn."

She was silent for a moment. "Vanaheim is not so bad in the autumn," she said finally. "I could live with you there at that time. And for the rest, I could spend the springtime in Alfheim, though I like it not, and I expect that the Alfar will like me little as well."

"I am not without power in Alfheim," Frey said, smiling. "They will treat you well, or hear from me about it."

"But in the spring," Gerda said, "I will go home to my family's hall, and you must go make peace with your hostage-masters, and we will be apart. There is no hope for that. I will never go to

Asgard." And Frey could see from the tilt of her chin that nothing could move her on this point, and so he agreed. It pained him to be caught between his oaths and her pride, but his love for her was great enough that being together for half the year was worth losing her for the other half.

She stood still again for a moment, as if she had not expected him to agree, as if she was only just realizing the full force and depth of his love for her, and she looked for a moment lost, like a girl who is unsure of what to say. Then he stepped close to her, and decided that the time had come to go beyond speaking, and he kissed her, and his golden aura enveloped her like the sun rising behind a dark standing stone. And soon her long cloak fell to the ground, and her dress pooled about her ankles, and they spent the night there together in the Barri Woods.

Just before dawn, as the sky was beginning to lighten, Gerda asked the one question that she had carried with her in her heart all these years. "What is it like, to die and return?" she asked him as they lay together under the trees.

"Cold," he said. "It is cold, and dark, and I walk the Hel-road, and every year the guardian says, 'Greetings, my lord. It is good to see you again.' And every year I am afraid that they will open the gate for me, but they always turn me back, and then I awaken to my body."

"Do you remember the pain after you awake?" she asked him.

"Always," he said, and kissed her.

When the sun rose, Gerda and Frey set sail in his magical ship to Jotunheim, where they landed on the shore near her father's hall, and Gerda took him to meet her family. Gymir looked upon the Vana-lord who would have his daughter's hand, and saw that he was scratched and bleeding, and smiling so brightly that he shone like the sun, and Gymir said, "I see that you have satisfied my daughter." And he laughed, and all his folk roared with laughter, but Frey laughed too just as loudly, and lifted his shirt to show his scratches, and this opened their hearts to him. Frey and

Gerda pledged their troth there, in front of Gymir and Aurboda, and the wedding was planned for a fortnight hence.

But there was one among them who did not laugh, and who indeed sat scowling through the ceremony. Afterwards, Beli went to Gerda and pulled her aside, and told her, "You bring shame on all of us by marrying outside your people."

Gerda pulled away and said, "I do not live my life for you, my brother, and I shall marry whom I choose." And she went away from him.

As she walked away, he called after her, "He is now my life-enemy, sister who values not her own kin! If it comes to war, I will kill him!" But she did not look back or speak to him, and indeed it was years before she spoke to him again.

After a fortnight of preparing, Gerda and Frey came forth to be married. A thousand guests of her father's attended from all corners of Jotunheim, and some came even from Niflheim, and gruff Surt the Black and some of his many sons came from Muspellheim. There were cliff-giants from the mountains, and frost-giants with snow still in their beards, and wolf-folk from the Iron Wood, and many others. The skin of a great cave-bear, which was the totem of Gymir's family, was spread before them and they stood upon it. Their hands were cut with knives and bound together, and the blood shared between them. "And now you are our family," said Gymir, "strange as it may seem. May you both be happy together, or at least not too miserable." And all the Jotnar howled for them, loud enough to shake the rafters of the hall.

Then they mounted the ship yet again, and Frey took Gerda home to Vanaheim, where he brought her before his mother Nerthus. "This is my beloved," he said to her, "whom I have married according to the custom of her people, and I would have you welcome her as a daughter."

"According to the custom of her people, perhaps," said Nerthus, "but if you wish me to welcome her as my daughter, you must be married according to the customs of your own people as well. I will not see any marriage to my son the Golden One unless it is with the wheat-wreaths and the burning grain." So Frey and Gerda had a second wedding, and the Vanir came from far and wide to watch them, and his sister Freya came and embraced Gerda.

"I am overjoyed to see my brother so happy again," she said. "He has loved no one like this before, in all the days of his life. Indeed, we thought that no one could capture his heart! Yet here you are, and I do not have to fear for him any more. I will welcome you as my sister, if you will have me, daughter of Gymir."

Gerda wondered at this, and said, "Tell me, Love Goddess of the Vanir: Why did your brother choose me, when he could have had any woman of your people, or of the Aesir?"

Freya embraced her and said, "Love strikes where it will, and who knows this better than I? I do not begrudge him his marriage, though it be to golden Vanir or proud Aesir or fey Alfar-maid or bearded Duergar-woman, or yet to a tall and beautiful etin-bride. Love is love, and it is always good."

And on the morrow they were awoken by singing, and when they came forth from Nerthus's house, the Vanir crowned them with wreaths of wheat, and laid sheaves of wheat in their hands, and drew them forth singing into the winter fields where a great fire was burning, and their hands were bound together, and

Gerda's braids were unbound and her long hair wrapped around Frey's shoulders. Bowls of grain were given to them to pour into the fire as an offering, and then gold rings were given to them to place on each others' fingers. They were taken to a bower made in a hollowed-out hayrick, and while they had a second wedding-night, the Vanir sang sweetly all around them.

The next morning, Frey said to his twice-wedded bride, "I fear that there must be a third wedding, for the folk of Asgard will not respect you as my wife unless we are married before them as well. And I will not have them say that you are some passing fancy that I will likely put aside when I am tired of you."

"But I have told you," Gerda said, "that I will never go to Asgard." And they parted in silence, with kisses and tears, and Frey went back to fulfill his oath, and Gerda returned to her family at Gymir's hall, where she sat silent in the wintry garden and stared at the withered herbs.

Her mother comforted her, and told her that many women went without their husbands; some were wed to sailors, or travelers, or men with other wives or families. It was not uncommon for giants to have more than one wife or husband, and to live apart. "Perhaps you should take a second husband, to comfort you when your golden lord is away," she suggested.

But Gerda shook her head. "I have seen no one I wish to wed," she said, and would say no more about it.

For himself, Frey was quieter than usual, and he did not join in the revelry of Asgard, and he was often seen to sigh to himself. But he took up again his duties and no longer lay weeping in his bed, and many of the folk of Asgard considered him cured of what had ailed him. However, gossip travels with a will of its own, and Skirnir's tongue was by no means discreet, so it was not long before all of Asgard knew that Frey had secretly married an etin-woman. So it was that Odin and Frigga called Frey forth to Gladsheim, and he came, knowing what it was they would ask.

It was Frigga who spoke first, as he knew that she would; marriage was her realm. "My lord Frey," she asked him, "we hear that you have wooed the daughter of an etin-lord. Tell us, do you intend to wed her, or is she merely a concubine you are visiting in Jotunheim?"

"I have already wed her, Lady," Frey said, "by the rituals of her people, and of mine. Gymir's daughter is my wife, and nothing shall change that."

At this a great clamor arose of many voices speaking at once. Some cried out against this union of Asa-sworn Van and Jotun lady; some cursed Frey for a fool; some said that at least there had been no wedding by their own customs, so it was no real wedding after all. One woman's mouth spoke forth that this was the known promiscuity of the Vanir, and that it had finally brought shame on them all.

At this, Freya stepped forth and chided the crowd. "Do you all scoff at the power of Love?" she demanded. "Love has done this, and I say that it is well done. There is little enough love in the world; do not condemn love that has sprung up unawares!" And saying this, she remembered her lost husband, and turned away in tears.

Frigga stood also, and held out her hands to both those who condemned and those who defended, and also those who stood silent. "Rather than letting this be a division between these worlds," she said, "let it be a bridge and a frithmaking between us." And Odin stood forth with his wife, and although some still muttered about the weak words of women, the clamor was silenced.

Odin turned to Frey. "We will welcome your bride, if she comes here," he said, "but as you are a sworn frith-guest of ours, you must marry her by our customs, in our city."

"That, my Lord Odin," said Frey, "will be entirely up to her."

The next day an Alfar lord and lady came to Frey and they spoke formally to him. "Lord Frey, you were set to watch and guard us by the Aesir, and we have long respected you, for you are a good and honorable man. But now we hear that you would take a giantess to wife, and we ask you not to do this, for it would bring shame upon you."

"Who I marry is none of your concern," Frey said. "I love this woman, and she shall be my wife, etin or no."

"My Lord, we beg you," protested the Alfar lord, "do not bring this giantess as your consort into our land! Do not force this bloodthirsty barbarian upon us!"

Frey smiled, thinking of Gerda, and how she had licked his scratches. "I shall do that," he said. "I shall bring my bloodthirsty barbarian etin-bride into your realm, and you will treat her with courtesy and hospitality, because I am the Guardian of Alfheim and I say it will be so." And though they pleaded with him, he would not hear them. And so it was that their marriage was condemned by as many as welcomed it, and from that time on any who would wed against the desires of their family or clan, or against the laws of their people, could call upon Frey and Gerda to bless their union.

In the meanwhile, while Gerda sat at her father's home, her cousin Skadi came to Gymir's hall. Skadi was a whirl of white furs and stomping boots, shaking snow off of her hood and doffing her doeskin gloves. "Greetings, Lady of the Snows!" cried Aurboda. "What brings you to Gymir's hall?"

Skadi's eyes lit on Gerda. "First, to congratulate my cousin on her wedding. Forgive me that I did not attend, but I was still in mourning for my late father Thjazi. Second, to tell you that I am going to Asgard to demand wergild for his death, and I hope to enter with my cousin when she goes to her husband."

"I have told my husband that I will not set foot in Asgard," Gerda said. "And what does your father's wergild have to do with me?"

Skadi's dark eyes gleamed. "It has much to do with you, my cousin. Why will you not go to Asgard? Do you not realize what a chance this is for your people?"

Gerda frowned at her, but the frost-giantess continued. "Those Aesir never let my father have a place in their council, even after he married one of them and inherited her land after she died! But they may let us speak, if we are married to some of them, because the Aesir underestimate their womenfolk. You are Frey's wife; you might have a chance to get your people's voice heard there in the White World. Why do you pass up this chance?"

"But you are no one's wife, Skadi," said Aurboda. "What is your plan?"

Skadi smiled coolly. "Why, I shall go and claim the property of my father and stepmother, and I shall ask for wergild for my father's death. I shall appeal to Tyr, and I expect that he will say my request is fair. And as wergild, I shall ask One-Eye for a husband. The Aesir believe that womenfolk all need fathers and husbands to protect them; they will believe the request." She threw back her head and laughed, shaking snow everywhere.

"But then you will have to marry whoever Odin chooses," Gerda said. "My husband is kind and beautiful; what if yours is not?"

"Then I will divorce him after a reasonable time," Skadi said, "and by then my voice will be well established there. Besides, I hear that Frigga's youngest is most handsome, and perhaps I will get lucky." She rubbed her hands together. "Come with me, cousin; we shall be as sisters there, and keep each other company, I promise."

Gymir stepped forward and touched his daughter's shoulder. "I would not force you to leave my household," he said, "but Skadi speaks wisdom. They would never let a warrior onto the council there who was not sworn to them, but you are a bride, and they would not see you as a warrior but as a wife; such are their ways. You could speak for your people."

So it was that Gerda dwelt on the matter for some days, and finally she agreed to go to Asgard, though her heart was heavy. And a message was sent to Frey, who rejoiced and began to make ready for their third wedding day.

But Skadi went ahead, in her snowy sleigh, armed with weapons and clad in her best snow-white furs, and railed for wergild at the gates of Asgard. And, as the tale goes, Odin allowed her to claim her inheritance of land, although no bloodline gave it to her, and he placed all the unmarried Aesir men in a circle around her. She allowed herself to be blindfolded, and was told that she must touch the feet of the men, and choose one only by their feet. So she chose the one that she felt had the best-formed feet, and lo and behold when the blindfold was removed she stared into the face of Njord the Vanir Lord of seafaring, the father of Gerda's husband Frey. And all the Aesir men breathed a sigh of relief, for they had feared to be forcibly married by Odin's word to the forbidding giantess. Skadi was a little disappointed that she had not chosen the beautiful Baldur, but Njord was a handsome man, and clearly kind of heart, so she was content enough with the way things had gone.

The next day, when Gerda came to Asgard, Frey kissed her in front of all of them, and said, "This is my beloved, and let no one speak against her." And Freya stood with them and spoke for them, and Frigga came forth to speak of frith and peacemaking and the sacredness of marriage vows, and finally Odin spoke forth and blessed their union, and no others spoke out publicly against them. And it came to pass that Gerda married Frey on the same day that Skadi married his father, and they placed their hands on Frigga's spindle and walked under Odin's spear, and there was feasting and dancing for days. Thrice-wedded, they went to their third wedding night as if it was their first.

Gerda tried to make herself at home in Asgard, and Freya gave her a walled courtyard at Sessrumnir to plant the cloistered herb gardens that she loved. Many of the Aesir were courteous to her, and came to value her, but though none dared mutter against her in her hearing, she heard many of them curse her kin, and her race, and speak ill of them. And Gerda was silent, for it was not her way to do battle in public over the words of others.

She finally spoke to her husband about it, but he bade her to ignore their hard words, and to remember that they were not speaking against her. Still, it ate at her heart, and she felt that an insult to her kin, or to her race, spoken in her presence, was indeed an insult to her. The months drew on, and she did not feel at home, and began to long for a place where she did not have to guard her tongue so. And after a long time of this, she discovered something that made her troubled heart weep, something she had forgotten until it came upon her.

So Gerda went to her husband and drew him into her walled garden, in the night while the stars shone down upon them. And she sat with him on the bench where they had sat many times before, and laid her hand upon his knee, and said to him: "There is life in my womb, heart of my heart. We have quickened us a child."

And Frey cried out in joy and would have embraced her, but she held him away from her and said, "I tell you this not as tidings of happiness, but of sorrow. For when our child comes of age, to whom shall he be forced to swear fealty? If battle should be called, what side will he be on? What geas shall be laid upon him before he is even born?"

Frey was silent, and then said, "As my father swore to be a hostage to the Aesir, so he swore also for his children, and their children and grandchildren. So I am hostage, and my sister Freya, though not our half-sisters who have other fathers. And Freya's daughters are also so bound, and so would be my children."

Gerda placed her hands over her womb in a gesture like an iron gate, and said, "I will not bear children to be hostages to anyone's whim. I will not give them life only to take away their freedom, especially as they have my blood in them, and will be scorned by many."

"Yet I cannot fulfill my oath otherwise," said Frey. "What would you have me do, my love? For this is your womb, and your decision. That is the way of the Vanir."

Then it was her turn to be silent, until finally she said, "If this is how it must be, then I will bear you no children at all. I will not have them torn between loyalties that they did not choose. I will still this life in my womb, and I will bear no more until there is peace between all our peoples."

Frey heaved a sigh. "That day may never come."

"Then I shall remain barren," said Gerda. And he embraced her in silence, and they both wept, but that night she gathered certain herbs from her garden and brewed them into a brew, and stilled the life within her womb. And so it came to pass that the Lord of Life, who gives such growth to the fields and flocks, has a barren marriage, and that Gerda turns often to her herbs to ensure that it is so, and that many women who need also to still the quickening life within them turn to her for aid and ease of passage.

And after having lived many years in Asgard, Gerda made ready to leave and go to her home in Jotunheim, for she did not feel that she could stay there any longer. She told her husband that she would meet him in his hall in Alfheim, and his home in Vanaheim when he was allowed to come home, and that he would always be welcome in her father's hall in Jotunheim. They wept again, and embraced, and parted, telling each other that their love would endure even such a yearly parting, and promising to see each other in the summer.

Gerda packed quietly, and would have left Asgard with no one knowing, yet Skadi got wind of it and came to her as she was clipping sprigs of herbs to take with her. "You would abandon me here in the White World, then, my cousin?" she asked.

"It grieves my heart sore," Gerda said, "but I must go. I cannot live among the killers of my kin and the haters of my race, though we both agreed to make this sacrifice. My sacrifice will be different, though."

"Then if you must go and leave me alone as the sole voice for Jotunheim," Skadi said to her, "I charge you with this: When our people come into councils, speak for me. Remind them why they sent me here, and why we work for peace against all odds. Be my voice, not that of your family. Do this for me, your cousin alone in the White World."

"Alone?" asked Gerda. "Is your husband, the father of my own beloved, not to your taste, my cousin?'

"His hall is not to my taste," said Skadi. "For the mewing of the gulls and the noise of the sea awakens me too early, and I stink of salt air. And he will not dwell far from the sea; my mountains make him long for the waters. He is a pleasant enough fellow, but we shall have to live apart for much of the year. So it seems, my sister, that we shall both be absent brides... but my place here is now assured, and my voice will speak for our race, if you will speak for me."

"I will do this," Gerda said to her, and they embraced, and Gerda went forth from Asgard and never returned. She kept her word, speaking for Skadi in the councils of Thrym, and she spent the winter with her family in the snow, and then went forth to Vanaheim in the summer, much as she had gone forth so long ago as a young maid, to see the Golden One die by the hand of the priestess of the Vanir, and to welcome him back to life with kisses when he arose again.

Gerda Prayer Beads
Raven Kaldera

These were made as a small set to match Frey's beads. Where his are mostly golden and sparkling, hers are in earth tones. Instead of the seasons, hers mark the Anglo-Saxon months.

(Large Unakite Bead)
Hail Gerda, Lady of the Walled Garden!

(Green And Black Nut Bead)
May you guard my heart from all harm.

(Green And Black Nut Bead)
May you guard my hands from all mischief.

(Green And Black Nut Bead)
May you guard my hearth from all despair.

(Snowflake Obsidian Bead)
In the month of the Wolf, you hide the home from all predators.

(Mottled Agate Bead)
In the month of the covering snows, you cradle the waiting seed.

(Brown Ceramic Chinese Bead With Butterflies)
In the month of the great winds, you walk gently on the bare earth.

(Light Green Jasper Bead)
(In the month of the spring's opening, you welcome the first green.

(Dark Green Jasper Bead)
In the month of the milk cow, you grow the garden high.

(Moss Agate Bead)
In the month of the high sun, you wait for your beloved.

(Large Unakite Bead)
Hail Gerda, Lady of the Walled Garden!

(Green And Black Nut Bead)
May you guard my heart from all harm.

(Green And Black Nut Bead)
May you guard my hands from all mischief.

(Green And Black Nut Bead)
May you guard my hearth from all despair.

(Brown Jasper Bead)
In the month of haying, you weed away what is no longer necessary.

(Amber Glass Faceted Bead)
In the month of the falling grain, you watch your beloved go to the knife.

(Green Glass Faceted Bead)
In the month of mead-making, you welcome the Golden One back from the dark.

(Mahogany Obsidian Bead)
In the month of warning winds, you harvest the roots from deep in the earth.

(Blood-Red Glass Bead)
In the month of blood, you hallow the life that does not come to fruition.

(Green and White Jasper Bead)
In the month of the darkening Sun, you bring frith to the halls of others.

(Large Unakite Bead)
Hail Gerda, Lady of the Walled Garden!

(Green And Black Nut Bead)
May you guard my heart from all harm.

(Green And Black Nut Bead)
May you guard my hands from all mischief.

(Green And Black Nut Bead)
May you guard my hearth from all despair.

A Prayer to Frey and Gerda For Harmony In Marriage
Raven Kaldera

Hail to Frey who loved so fiercely
That he gave up his sword for love
And went to his beloved unarmed.
Hail to Gerda who took a risk
On love, and won great happiness
By being willing to be open.
Hail to the wedded pair over whom
Nine worlds shook their heads,
All people cried out in their skepticism
That this would never last,
That this was never proper.

Teach us to go to each other
Without weapons in our hands,
The blades of tongues, the spears
Of words, the arrows of angry deeds.
Teach us to go to each other
Without walls of flame to guard,
Without shields to hide our needs,
Without masks to hide our thoughts.
Teach us that our hearth is sacred
No matter who watches, no matter
What fingers are pointed, what sharp
And contemptuous words are said.
Teach us that we need not be ashamed
When storms arise, for they arise for all.

Hail to the Beloved Gods who smile
Upon us as we struggle. I beg you,
Lend your hands to the work of frith
In home and hearth and marriage bed
As well as tribe and clan, for one

Breeds peace or war with the other.
Hail to the Gods of Love That Lasts
And may our love survive as long
And as steadily as a standing stone
In the wake of the storm.

Frey and Gerda Wedding Blessing
Raven Kaldera

Since weddings are highly personal affairs, rather than creating a Frey-and-Gerda-based wedding ritual, I have chosen simply to include an opening invocation and a closing blessing which can be integrated into any wedding ritual.

Wedding Invocation
Hail Frey, Golden God of the Vanir,
Hostage and ally of the Aesir,
Wedded in alliance with the Jotnar,
You reach across boundaries
And extend your hands in peace,
Showing that Love can conquer all obstacles,
Showing that Love can encompass all lines
Drawn by outsiders to keep safe their fears,
Showing those boundaries for the illusions
That they most certainly are.
You who gave up your sword for love,
You who gave up your steed for friendship,
You who went defenseless and open
To an uncertain meeting, hoping and believing
That love would make all things right.
Hail Frey, Golden God of the Vanir,
Be with us on this day when we gather
To watch these lovers be united.

Hail Gerda, daughter of Gymir,
Giantess, goddess of the Walled Garden,
Fiercely guarding what is yours,
Keeping your thoughts, your feelings
Close to your stone-strong heart.
Mountain goddess, earth daughter,
Keeper of the roots and herbs,

You hold with love and faithfulness
To your lord Ingvi, even though
Your union sparked debate and hate
On every side, still you held strong.
Even when you cannot be at his side,
Still you are steadfast in your heart.
Even when you must see him be cut down
And do what is necessary, you weep
But never regret, for you understand
That Love is worthy of all obstacles.
Hail Gerda, Etin-bride and guardian,
Be with us on this day when we gather
To watch these lovers be united.

Wedding Blessing

As Frey and Gerda love each other forever
And are eternally newlywed, despite all time,
May you always lick honey from each others' fingers
And savor the honey of each others' hearts.
Like the Gods who love despite all disapproval,
May you never let the words of others
Make you swerve in any way from your love.
Like the Gods who will not bear children to be hostage,
May you be able to make hard decisions together,
And may those hard decisions not divide you,
But bring you closer in mutual comfort.
Like the Gods who love beyond all reason,
May you likewise love beyond all reason
And may your love be grounded in the Earth,
Like Vanir soil, like Jotnar mountain stone.
Hail to the Gods of Wedded Bliss
And may their blessings spill forth upon you.

Autumn Equinox Recipes for a Frey Feast

Wild Boar
Seawalker

Ingredients:
1 2-pound leg of wild boar, if you can get it—specialty meat shops or hunters may be able to help, even if you're in America—wild pigs are getting out of hand and backbreeding to boar status in many southern states.

1 onion, chopped
3 garlic cloves, crushed
1 small carrot, chopped
1 celery stalk, chopped
2 cups red wine
6 tablespoons red wine vinegar
1 bay leaf
4 whole mustard seeds
4 black peppercorns
4 juniper berries
8 bacon slices, diced
½ cup pork stock
Salt
1 tbsp. cornstarch
½ cup cream
A handful of wild mushrooms, sautéed in butter

This is not a quick dish due to the extensive marinating, so plan accordingly. Clean and rinse the boar meat and lay it in a large pot. Mix the vegetables, wine, and spices and pour over the meat. Cover and refrigerate, and let the meat marinate for between 1 and 3 days. When done, remove meat and set marinade aside. Sauté bacon and melt butter in the pot, put the meat back, and brown the meat on all sides. Pour in the pork stock and some of the marinade. Cover and cook for 2 hours or until tender. Turn it periodically, pouring more marinade over the top if necessary. When done, put the cooking liquid (removing the bay leaf) into a saucepan. Mix the cream and cornstarch, then stir slowly into the cooking liquid until thickened. Stir the wild mushrooms into the sauce and serve with the wild boar meat.

Borscht (for Gerda, who loves root vegetables)
Raven Kaldera

Ingredients:
6 large beets, chopped (or the equivalent in smaller beets)
1 pound pork sausage
3 grated carrots
1 onion, chopped fine
1 small red cabbage, grated
4 cloves garlic, chopped fine
1 tbsp. butter
2 quarts water
Salt and pepper
Sour cream to top it with

Peel all the beets. Chop half of them coarsely and the rest slice and chop finer. Salt the water and bring it to a boil; cook the coarsely chopped beets until they entirely lose their color. Pull them out and discard them (we give them to the chickens). Then put in the rest of the beets, carrot, and cabbage and let them cook, but only until tender—check frequently. Meanwhile, cook the sausage meat in a skillet and set aside. Melt the butter in the skillet and fry the onions and garlic, then put them in the pot as soon as the veggies are tender. Stir, serve, and add sour cream as a garnish.

Frey's Nutcake (Gluten Free)
Seawalker

Ingredients:
1 ½ cups chestnut flour
½ cup softened butter
½ tsp. baking powder
½ tsp. baking soda
½ tsp. salt
¼ cup chopped walnuts
¼ cup chopped almonds or hazelnuts
3 eggs, separated
½ cup honey
2 tbsp. sugar
Honey-soaked nuts, if desired

This is an egg-white cake, so handle it carefully. Roast all the nuts in the oven, get off all skins, and chop fine. Mix the dry ingredients and stir in the nuts. Mix the butter, honey, and egg yolks and beat until smooth. Add the dry mixture and beat it in thoroughly. Whip the egg whites until stiff, adding the sugar a little at a time. Fold into the cake mix a little at a time. Bake in a round greased pan for 30-45 minutes at 350 degrees until done— you may want to cover the cake top with foil for the last 15 minutes. Sprinkle with powdered sugar and decorate with honey-soaked nuts.

Harvest King

Prayer for the Harvest King
Ari

The last of harvest comes into the home,
The final bushels pass the threshold stone,
The grain is cut, the stubble in the fields
Reminds us of the bounty of our yields.
He is in every root and loaf and sheaf,
He is in each saved seed and drying leaf,
He is the cherished hopes we secret save,
To plant next spring in each their earthen grave.
God of the Ancestors, Lord of the Mound,
Whose people here are gathered all around,
We hail you as your golden fades to brown,
We know it was for us that you went down.

Golden God, Golden Crown: Frey and Kingship
Gudrun of Mimirsbrunnr

When we think of Norse or Germanic myths solely in terms of the cosmology, Frey is not generally recognized as a king. After all, his land—Vanaheim—is ruled by his father Njord, or (more likely) his mother Nerthus. He is a prince, perhaps, but not directly a ruler. Step away from the simple cosmology, however, and Frey is often bound up with kingship in the accounts of his worship. He was known in Old Norse as *höfdingi* (chieftain), *fólkvaldi goða* (people's divine ruler), and *folkum stýrir* (people's guide). The royal families of Sweden counted descent from him, as the Ynglings. As a divine ancestor of royalty, he conferred blessings upon his ruling descendants.

Northern kings were supposed to be fountains of magical fertility, as the King's bond with the land he ruled was sacral as well as civil. Legends abound of kings praying to the land and having springs come forth from the earth, or seeds leap forth magically into grain—powers that could only come from the Gods of Fertility.[6] It is the King's sacred duty, first and foremost, to feed his people. If they starve, there will be nothing left, so that King becomes a kind of high priest whose job it is to wake the land and spur it to higher yields. In other parts of ancient Europe and Eurasia, kings publicly copulated with mares, or cows, or a priestess who symbolized the earth in order to magically stimulate fertility.

Kings were also felt to be a mobile point of great power, specifically the power of the law made tangible, *mikill griþastaþr*— a place of great peace. As such, it is not surprising that in Iceland outlaws were forbidden to enter a temple to Frey. Their presence disrupted not only Frey's peace, but Frey's lawful energy as well. [7] The second sacred duty of a King, after food, is of course the

---

[6] Wright, P.E. *The Cultivation of Saga in Anglo-Saxon England.* Edinburgh Press, 1939.

[7] Chadwick, H.M. *The Origin of the English Nation.* Cambridge, 1924.

keeping of the peace. The euhemeristic Norse Kings that are associated with Frey (and some thought to be byforms or the origins of Frey)—Frodhi, Olaf Geirstadhaalfr, Halfdan the Black—were spoken of as having reigns of decades of peace and fertile seasons, and after their deaths their burial mounds became places of worship and miracles.

In English Saxon lore, the myths of kingship passed from Pagan to Christian symbolism, but still retained for a long while the sacred wheatsheaf. As the scion of the Grain God, handing over a wheatsheaf to the King tied him still further to the fertility and good seasons that his reign would hopefully bring. It is notable that West Saxon royalty descended from the ancient kings Scyld and Sceaf (Shield and Sheaf).[8] While Christianity eventually took over entirely, the name of Frey became, for a time during the transitional period, simply another name for the Christian God. In Old English we see *lifes frea, heofona frea, engles frea, rices frea*; in *The Dream Of The Rood*, we read *Geseah ic tha frean mancynnes* (I saw there the "Frey" of mankind). As a sacrificed god, Christ and Frey may have blended for a time, and the kingship descended from both during that uncertain period.

Boars, too, were kingship symbols among the Norse—King Heidrek takes his oaths on the sacrificial "atonement boar" in *Heidrek's Saga*. Another symbol of northern kingship was the stag, peripherally associated with Frey as sacrificed god, as he defends himself with a stag's antler at Ragnarok. The stag was associated with the new year and the new King, and fertility-god rites were mixed into those symbols.

We use the term "sacrificial King" over and over again, without too much thought as to what it means. There is plenty of debate on the issue of whether the original position of "King" was one that the individual was not meant to survive; i.e. that Kings were allowed to rule for a short time and then sacrificed. That

---

[8] Chaney, William. *The Cult of Kingship in Anglo-Saxon England.* Manchester University Press, Manchester, UK. 1970

theory claims that eventually the King decided that he didn't wish to give up his throne to death, and instead chose a King-sacrifice who would die in his stead. The legendary king Aun or Ani of Uppsala sacrificed each of his nine sons, one at a time, instead of himself and eventually died of old age. Other Uppsala kings— Domaldi and Olaf Tree-feller—were slain by their people as a sacrifice when the hoped-for "good seasons" did not arrive.[9] We forget that kings could be killed, in those times, if they did not magically produce the Freylike qualities that were required of them. The step from sacral to sacrificial king was a small one in those days.

It seems that Frey's connection with kingship, then, is not so much that he is a king as that he is the power that grants a successful kingship to mortals—plenty, peace, and no need to sacrifice anyone. As with all divine gifts, these can be withdrawn. When that happens, the King must accept the other, more terrible gift of Frey—the ability, when all else fails, to bring back prosperity with one's own life's blood. Frey offers this choice to the one who would hold the life and death of the people in his hand, showing that the King is not above that choice of life or death, but is the linchpin that holds the sacrificial magic in place.

---

[9] Sheffield, Ann Groa. *Frey, God of the World.* Lulu.com 2007.

Freyr: A Man to Man Rite
Dokkulfr

Even before I knew I was a Yngling, I knew I was Vaningi. I don't know when he first made his presence felt, only that among all the Northern Gods, He and His sister went right to my heart. Maybe They chose me because I was Wiccan then; they are, after all, an archetypal Lord and Lady pair ... but only They know for sure. Even then, the Northern tradition pulled at me.

My initiating priest's patron was Thor. I knew some of the Runes, and Loki had made his presence known in a major way ... but as I look back, I'm quite amused by Frey's choice in me. My mother had terrible taste in men. So as I dealt with these "excuses" for men, I began to formulate an opinion on masculinity, and not a fond one ... which is ironic, as I am bisexual. But it wasn't until later, seeking the true love and acceptance of my own masculinity, that I began to realize that Ingvi held a standard that I could, and would, be proud to uphold.

Ingvi-Freyr exemplifies what I believe masculinity should look like: Love, Frith, Sacrifice, Beauty, Passion. The following is a rite acknowledging, accepting, and committing to the example our Lord set for us.

You Will Need:
A piece of deer antler
A bowl of water with honey or mead mixed into it
A bowl of grain (oats, barley, or a mix of any)
The runes Jera and Ingwaz carved on a *taufr* (talisman)
A bunch of coltsfoot and fern fronds bound with green and gold cord, string or yarn (Optionally, a large phallus may be used.)
A green, gold or white candle, cherry-scented if you can find it
Incense (I personally use "Elfin Forest" by *Scents of Midnite*, but any evergreen, pine, cedar, lemon balm, cherry, etc. would be fine.)
A small bowl of honey
An offering bowl
Something made of gold

Note: Please attempt to ensure that, whenever possible, organic and chemical-free products are used.

This rite can be done any time of year, but Winternights feels right to me, allowing you to see your "harvest" in nine months. It could be incorporated as part of a Freyr's blot.

Facing west, I hold aloft the deer's antler and use it to trace an Earth/Solar shield-cross. I use the following pattern (I call this my "*Brisinga-Rûn* hallowing"): Trace a line from right to left, then curve up a quarter-circle. Then draw the line down, creating a sort of "flipped" Thor's Hammer, or a curved numeral four. Following that, complete a sunwise circle around the figure, forming the shield. [1]

Holding the antler aloft at a 45 degree angle in front of me, I say: "Horni Vestri, Helga vé þetta ok hald vorþ!" (Horn I hold West, hallow and keep this space holy!) I proceed North, East, and South (Norþri, Austri, Suþri) using the same formula, changing the direction names.

Upon completion of the hallowing of the space, I face West and say: "Eg Kalla viðhinn afl frá eftir Freyr!" (I call upon the strength of Freyr!)[2] I pause to feel his presence and his power. Then, having connected with Him, I proceed to my altar and retrieve the honeyed water and my asperger. Starting in the West, I sprinkle my vé with the "mead", seeing the golden drops nourishing the land and its vaettir. When I finish "feeding" the space, I light the candle and incense.

I then move the offering bowl (I use one inside; outdoors I offer to the earth itself) close to the front, setting the honey-bowl left, the grain right, and the gold above. I recite a short ode of praise to Him.

Ode To Ingvi-Freyr

I hail thee, Golden God, Lord of my soul and kin.
Verðanði Goð, Lord of the Fields, my light within.

Ingvi-Freyr, my heart sings each day,
The taste of your name on my lips,
The touch of your love, it's funny how you fill me.

I call to Elf-Home, your abode,
As I walk with you along the road.
Walk along my side.
Show me the way to honor and frith,
My only wish for your example to shine within me.

Masculine like no other, a level to inspire!
Always generous, never callous,
Sacrificing sword and steed for those you love,
God with erect phallus!

Father of my line, Yngling am I,
My blood calls to you,
You who sired my Ancestors.

Gift me with power, lead me to honor and right,
Come and fill me as I follow your light.

After completing the praise-ode portion of the rite, I grab the taufr and hold it in my hand. Focusing on Ingvi-Freyr and mentally recounting the examples I wish to embody, I close my eyes and speak to Him. By now I can usually feel his presence. I say:

Freyr! My Lord! Example of Love, Sacrifice, and Frith! I call to you! Strengthen my will to love and sacrifice like You. Give me the strength to fight without steel, teach me dignity, compassion, and manners befitting royalty. Show me the way to reap the riches of my soul's harvest. Show me the way of stewardship for all life and love. Teach me to sow for the future. Grant me virility like you and Gullinbursti possess. Teach me discretion and honor to accompany it!

I see to what ends Your example grows, and as I offer you this grain *(here place some grain in the bowl or offering place)* may I harvest the qualities of gentle masculinity. As I offer this honey *(pour some honey)* may my words and deeds be kind and sweet to those I love. As I offer this gold *(place gold in offering dish/place)* may I hold those I cherish as precious as You and You example.

I ask that you imbue this *taufr* with the qualities You embody. Grant me the privilege of your divine ecstasy. (Focus on his essence as it imbues the *taufr*.)

After I feel his essence infusing it, I place the taufr on my person in order to take the energy with me wherever I go. I then go to the altar and retrieve the mead bowl. Holding it high, I say: "My thanks to you, my Lord, for your presence. My life is left brighter for you bring me Right Order." I pour half of the mead into the offering bowl, then I take a drink, then I thank the Vaettir, pouring the rest out to them.

I walk to the West, and say: "I thank all the Gods of Vanaheim and all those allied with Freyr." Facing the center, I say: "I thank all the Vaettir, spirits and energies gathered here; wend your way as you will. I release the shield wall and any force trapped by my rite." And it is over.

Bibliography

Gundarsson, Kvedulf. *Our Troth V.1.* BookSurge Publishing, 2006.

Gundarsson, Kvedulf. *Teutonic Religion.* Thoth Publications, 2008.

Gundarsson, Kvedulf. *Teutonic Magic.* Thoth Publications, 2008.

Krasskova, Galina, and Kaldera, Raven. *Northern Tradition for the Solitary Practitioner.* New Page Press, Franklin Lakes, NJ, 2009

Thorsson, Edred. *Nine Doors of Midgard.* Runa-Raven Press, 2003.

Thorsson, Edred. *Witchdom of the True.* Runa-Raven Press, Smithville, TX, 1999

---

[1] The "Brisinga-Rûn Hallowing" was inspired by p. 52-53 of *Witchdom of the True* by Edred Thorsson (Smithville, TX: Runa-Raven Press 1999).

[2] Literally, "I call upon the power of Freyr." My own arrangement of Icelandic, which may be grammatically off.

Domestication as Sacred Contract

Joshua Tenpenny

On a deep spiritual level, our relationship with the living things around us forms a complex web of obligations and responsibilities. One of those fundamental relationships is our domestication of plants and animals. This is typically seen as a process of powerful humans exerting their will over passive and essentially helpless beings, but as an animist, I do believe there is consent and cooperation. A species cannot be domesticated without its consent, as you can see by the countless species which cannot be successfully domesticated.

I believe that each species has an overarching spirit of some sort, that goes beyond the consciousness of the individual plant or animal. This overarching spirit influences the behavior and form of the species, and it is the consciousness which drives evolutionary changes to that species. A human culture forms relationships with these overarching spirits through their interactions with the individual plants and animals, whether or not they also have an intentional direct relationship with that overarching spirit. These spirits have a very clear and unsentimental understanding of the cycles of life and death.

In their efforts to reproduce and flourish, some plants have developed particularly tasty nutritious bodies to entice animals (including humans) to eat them. It is their intention to be eaten. When human cultures have come across particularly tasty plants growing wild, they try to cultivate them to gain access to a larger and more consistent supply. There are some plants which refuse to cooperate with this, and can only be gathered wild. There are some who cooperate enthusiastically, developing into new species who are substantially more useful to humans.

Some plants seem to be of such marginal food value in their wild, uncultivated state that it is hard to imagine humans selectively breeding generation after generation of these plants unless they had some good reason to think this plant had substantial food potential. This is particularly curious in plants like cassava which are very poisonous unless thoroughly processed, and plants like corn which seem to have developed quite suddenly from a wild barely edible state to a much different domesticated state where they are incapable of reproduction in the wild. I don't mean to insult the ingenuity or perseverance of our ancestors, but my intuitive understanding is that there was some kind of spiritual communication which inspired these things. I believe the spirits of those soon-to-be-domesticated species intentionally and voluntarily offered themselves to the human culture, establishing a contract whereby the humans nourish and support the plants, and the plants nourish and support the humans.

With livestock animals, it is very much the same process. In the wild, these were prey animals. They have always been food. They understand this. It is all right with them. They have entered into relationship with humans, gaining protection from wild predators as well as a consistent and ample supply of food. The overarching spirits of these animals do not mind ending up as food, but they do mind suffering in the meantime. Up until recently, animals kept in substandard conditions would get sick and die. This is their means of ensuring a certain standard of treatment. Unfortunately, advances in modern medicine have allowed us to keep animals in increasingly unpleasant environments, administering a steady stream of antibiotics and other medications to prevent the deaths that would be the natural consequence of these living conditions. I consider this to be a breach of our sacred contract.

Another way in which we may have overstepped the boundaries of our contract is the direct genetic modification of plants and animals. Selective breeding provides a natural means of genetic modification, and leaves the overarching spirit of that animal with plenty of room to influence the outcome. The direct genetic modification seems coercive to me. Like the routine medicating of livestock, it is most troubling when it is used to raise these plants and animals under conditions that would kill the unmodified species. (Herbicide-tolerant plants, such as the "Roundup Ready" soybean, are especially problematic, because in addition to this coercion of the species, it leads to the increased use of stronger and stronger pesticides. The competing plants, the "weeds", have overarching spirits of their own, and are quite resourceful in adapting to the increasingly toxic environment. Since these plants are not putting their resources into food production, they can focus solely on reproduction and survival.)

But there are people who are going back to that sacred contract, whether they understand it in those terms or not. Joel Salatin of Polyface Farm bases his agricultural model on "...mimicking natural patterns on a commercial domestic scale [which] insures moral and ethical boundaries to human cleverness." [10] There is increasing public awareness of food production issues, from the environmental impact of pesticide, the rise of food-borne illness, awareness of farm workers' rights, concern about the humane treatment of animals, and many other issues. I recognize my point of view is a minority even within my religious community, but I do hope for solutions to these problems that treat these plants and animals as our partners in the food production process, rather than our property or our victims.

---

[10] http://www.polyfacefarms.com/principles.aspx

Planting a Frey Garden
Raven Kaldera

My farm is dedicated to Frey. The land itself is Hela's, as is the house and all the back acreage; the herb garden is Gerda's, but the small 6-acre piece in the front that pastures animals and grows vegetables belongs to Frey. We aren't self-sufficient by any means, and any commercial farmer would laugh at us, but we manage to grow a significant portion of our meat, dairy, and vegetables without leaving home. I often plant seeds in the shapes of runes in the vegetable beds—Berkana, Inguz, Jera.

While Gerda is, for me, the goddess of the herb garden, and Frey is more specifically the deity of agricultural processes, not everyone has a farm or even a large vegetable garden. Some people aren't interested in growing their own food, or don't have the space, or the ability to do manual labor. If you do want to take part in (or at least support) agriculture but don't own land or live in a rural area, I strongly suggest that you get involved with a CSA (Community Supported Agriculture) farm. CSA farms will sell you a share of the harvest in advance, and you get deliveries of vegetables all summer. Most have working shares where your labor can buy your food, most are organic, and all encourage volunteering. You know where your food comes from, you support small farms, and because there is no middleman you get your veggies cheaper. CSA shares can also be given to those who can't afford them, as an offering to Frey. However, if you have a small plot (or a few planters) and you'd like to create a ritual garden bed for Frey, the following plants are favorites of his.

First I want to emphasize, for those who care, that the associations of specific plants with Frey are solely and only the result of me working with hundreds of herbs and vegetables, and continually asking various deities, "All right, which ones are yours? Is anyone particularly interested in this plant?" as well as asking plant-wights "Are there any Gods that you work with in these pantheons?" The latter, especially, yielded remarkably efficacious results. With the exception of grains, as far as I know there are no extant sources about which herbs Frey is fond of, but my personal gnosis has served me well here.

To start with, any grains will do, even tiny plots or large pots of them. Barley is the best, but rye, wheat, and oats work too. If you can find *Einkhorn hornemanii,* that's the original Neolithic proto-wheat of the ancestors, and it can be grown as a devotional activity. Even if you only grow a potful, cut it down at Lammas and tie it into a sacred sheaf.

Lemon Balm (*Melissa officinalis*) is the first herb that I think of when I think of Frey plants. It was a few solitary Heathens who mentioned to me that they used Lemon Balm for his incense, and it made perfect sense—it's clean, bright, and an anti-depressant. I've used it to call on Frey, as well.

The annual plant Carline Thistle (*Carlina acaulis*) was known as "boar's thistle" or "boar's throat", and as such is Frey's plant as Master of Gullinbursti. It's one of the only thornless thistles that I know of. (How like him—a thornless thistle!) Its modern name comes from Charlemagne's Thistle, as it was a medicinal favorite of the Emperor's.

Coltsfoot (*Tussilago farfara*) is sacred to Frey is his aspect as protector of farm animals, as it has an affinity with all hoofed beasts.

Hops (*Humulus lupulus*) is a hardy vine whose flower-pollen is used in brewing; sleeping on hop-stuffed pillows brings peace and good sleep, and in some traditions fertility and sexual energy.

If you want to grow a simple flower garden, with modern ornamental flowers that may not have any historical association with Frey, but you'd like to dedicate them to him, choose yellow/gold annuals. The color honors him as the Golden God, and their annual nature honors his cycle of yearly death and rebirth. In fact, you might want to go out on Lammas and cut off all the flowers, and put them in an arrangement on the Lammas altar. If some of them bloom again in a week or so, consider it a good omen from him.

Cherry trees are the tree that I associate most with Frey, and one could plant one of the dwarf cherry varieties even in a tiny garden. If you have a full-sized herb garden, of course, it's Gerda who you'll want to call on for advice and aid, and she has her own herbs ... but of course she's happy to see a Frey plot bedded down, as it were, in her garden. (For a Gerda tree, there is a purplish-black elder now on the market with the variety name "Gerda". I had to get one for her.)

Nut trees are also Frey's province, as nuts are sacred to him. While most of these may be too large for a garden, they could surround a garden as protection, so long as they don't overshadow things. A dwarf almond might be able to live in the middle of a garden, though. Nut trees take a long time to grow, but they are worth it for the eventual harvest. When you crack them, think of him.

Gerda, his bride, likes herbs such as the weedy Cleavers *(Galium aparine)* and the more delicate Lady's Bedstraw *(Galium verum)*, both of which are invasive and need to be kept in check. She also likes the dainty and useful Hyssop (Hyssopus officinalis), both the blue-flowered and the white varieties.

Beyla, Frey's servant and beekeeper, is said to enjoy Catnip *(Nepeta cataria)*, but if you want to honor her, simply planting a bee garden will do—perhaps with a Catnip plant in the center.

Should you want to put in anything for Frey's sister, Freya's special tree is Linden, and if you've seen a big Linden tree, you can believe it. Linden's leaves are a relaxant for stress relief. Freya is associated with beans, and you can grow ornamental beans such as Scarlet Runner Beans or Hyacinth Beans in the garden, or just ordinary favas which are lovely enough on their own when they flower, and useful as well. Other flowers that she was associated with are Cowslip (*Primula vulgaris*, whose flowers were said to be keys to Sessrumnir) and her cousin Primrose *(Primula veris)*, Strawberries, Daisies, Lily of the Valley, Snowdrops (said to be her tears at first being a hostage in Asgard), and the scarlet Pimpernel *(Anagallis arvensis)*.

Prayer to Frey, God of the Body

Michaela Macha

Frey, God of the body as well as of the soul,
teach me to become better friends with my body.
Often I ignore it, or do not fulfill its needs properly.
Yes, sometimes I am angry at it for hampering me.
Then I forget that without a body, I would not be here at all.
I would not have breath to say this prayer to you.
I would not be able to enjoy food, or drink,
and all the other gifts of the earth that my senses enjoy.
You provide me everything my body needs to survive,
and with more good things that make life worth living.
Remind me to take as good care of my body as of my spirit,
each in its own measure and according to its needs.

Samhain Ritual for Frey: Harvest King
Raven Kaldera

This is a ritual for a household, or a larger community, but it is especially geared to farmers, or people who keep gardens, or who preserve their own food. It is a blessing of the harvest for the year. Participants should ideally bring some sort of homegrown produce from their gardens, or jars of homemade jam, or the like. People who do not grow or preserve food should bring seasonal produce from local farms; even if you do not grow your own, you still eat the bounty of those who do, and it is bought with the monetary harvest that you have earned.

The altar should be decorated in browns and deep golds, with a wooden bowl of earth, a loaf of homemade bread with the rune Jera baked into the top, and a horn of homemade or locally-brewed dark craft beer. Empty baskets should be laid out for the produce that will not be brought in containers, with space for those who bring their own baskets. Other props include a drum, three "corn dollies" (abstract woven straw decorations, preferably spiraling) representing the Nornir, a "corn dolly" that represents Frey (we have one that is vaguely phallic with two bunches of wheat for testicles) and a wreath of autumn leaves with trailing ribbons of brown and deep gold. Even dried leaves will do, if you live in an area where the leaves have already gone by at Samhain.

If you or anyone in your group has the skill, you might think about making your own corn dollies. They are a traditional harvest craft, woven from the last bunch of grain cut from the fields. There are numerous books available on making them, both the spiraling hornlike sorts and the flat fanlike versions with fluffy curves of grain heads. Woven straw ornaments are also traditionally hung on Christmas trees in German and Scandinavian countries, but they were originally a harvest charm. Farmers hung them over doors and windows for good luck in next year's planting. Giving them out as part of the ritual is a nice touch if you can make enough. If you want to do it really authentically, you can grow a few square feet of your own grain and harvest it just for that purpose. Barley is traditional and has the most dramatic heads, but any grain will do. If you are really ambitious, grow *Einkorn hornemanii*, the original Neolithic ancestor of wheat which is still found in some specialty seed catalogs.

If there will be people present who do not drink alcohol—children, people in recovery, people with health issues, etc.—make it a matter of hospitality to have another horn or a cup filled with some nonalcoholic beverage that represents the harvest, such as fresh-pressed cider or juice. When it is time to pass the drink, if there are two kinds of drink, it's easiest to designate someone to be the "cup-bearer" beforehand and walk around the circle with the two cups, so that people can choose and not feel pressured or unwelcome. If they want neither, let them know that they can kiss the cup and pass it on, or if the rite takes place outside, pour a few drops onto the ground.

The officiant begins to beat the drum with a slow, steady rhythm, and calls out to the people:

Come before the altar of the Harvest King!
What we have sowed, we have now reaped,
And what we have reaped must carry us
Through the hardest winter.
Tonight, our beloved Frey is the Harvest King
Who blesses all that has been grown in His name
That we may have bounty at the next springtime.

Each participant brings forth the token of their season's harvest and lays it on the altar, saying: "Bless the harvest for which I have toiled, and may it feed me through the winter." When all the tokens have been laid on the altar, the officiant says:

Hail Frey, of the fertile earth
That grows your bounty to feed us.
Hail Frey, who dies that we might live,
And rises again, faithful as always.
Hail Frey, God of the Mound,
God of the Ancestors who watch over us,
Watching us take part in the cycle of life,
Of all that rises and falls again.
Hail Frey, Lord of Good Seasons,
May our future seasons also be as fine.

The officiant lays the wreath of leaves on top of the harvest tokens. The four corn dollies are brought forth, and laid one after another on the altar as the officiant says:

To that which has been, we are grateful!
To that which is, we are grateful!
To that which will become, we are grateful!
To the Harvest Lord, who paid for our full bellies,

We are grateful!
Now taste of the fruits of the harvest
And remember this gratitude, and be thou blessed.

The bread and horns of drink are passed around, while the officiant or another with a strong voice beats the drum and galdrs the rune Jera. The toasts are made in silence this time. At the end, the officiant recites the Prayer for the Harvest King, and dismisses the people. After they have feasted, they reclaim their blessed tokens of the harvest and take them home.

Samhain Recipes for a Frey Feast

Stuffed Red Cabbage Leaves
Seawalker

Ingredients:
1 medium head red cabbage
5 tbsp. butter
2 onions, chopped fine
1 cup breadcrumbs
1 pound ground pork
1 egg
Salt
¼ tsp dill weed
¼ tsp cumin
1 cup mushrooms
4 tbsp. flour
2 cups pork stock
1/3 cup cream

Clean the cabbage and remove the main stem. Boil a pot of salted water and plunge the cabbage in. After about 5 minutes, pull it out and remove the outer leaves, and repeat this until all the leaves have been removed. Melt 2 tbsp. butter in a saucepan and sauté half the onion. Put them in a bowl and stir in breadcrumbs, ground pork, egg, salt, and herbs. Flatten out each cabbage leaf gently, without breaking it, and pound the ribs gently flat with a wooden kitchen hammer. Divide the stuffing into 8 portions and place 1 portion on a large cabbage leaf. Roll it up, tucking the ends, and then roll that up in a second one. Repeat 7 more times. Melt the rest of the butter and sauté the cabbage rolls gently, turning them carefully. Remove them and add the rest of the onion and the mushrooms; sauté. Add the flour bit by bit, stirring as you go. Add the cream slowly, stirring constantly. Lay out the rolls in a serving dish and pour the sauce over them.

Frey's Rye Beer Bread

Seawalker

Ingredients:

1 12-oz. bottle of good yeasty beer—check craft beers until you find the right one.

½ tsp. honey

2 cups buttermilk

2 tsp. salt

1 tsp. ground cardamom

2 tsp. caraway seeds

4 cups whole wheat self-rising flour

3 cups rye flour

Grease a baking sheet and set aside. In a large bowl, mix the beer, honey, buttermilk, spices, and 2 cups of the whole wheat flour. Cover and set in a warm place for about an hour. Add the salt, rye flour, and enough whole wheat flour to make a soft, sticky dough. Turn it out onto a floured surface and knead it for about 10 minutes. Let it rise for half an hour and punch it down, let it rise for another half hour. Punch it down again and mold it into hemispherical loaves. Let rise for another half hour. Just before baking, cut an Inguz rune into the top with a butter knife. Bake at 400 degrees until done, at least an hour.

Onion Tart
Seawalker

Ingredients:
2 cups flour
2/3 cup warm milk
2 tsp. yeast
6 tbsp. butter
Pinch of salt
½ pound diced bacon, preferably thick-sliced
3 large onions, chopped fine
Pinch salt
¼ tsp. caraway seeds
4 eggs, beaten
1 cup sour cream

Add the yeast to the warm milk and let it get foamy, then stir in the flour and 2 ½ tbsp. softened butter and let it rise for half an hour. Punch it down, knead it for 10 minutes, then let it rise for another half hour. In the meantime, use ½ tbsp. butter to grease a large round pizza-style pan and set it aside. Melt the remaining butter and sauté the onions until they are clear, then in another skillet fry the bacon. Add the two together with the salt and caraway seeds.

Flatten the dough out onto the pizza pan as a base with pinched-up edges, and spread the onions and bacon on it. Mix the eggs into the sour cream and then slowly pour it over the onion mix. Bake for 40 minutes or until golden brown at around 350 degrees.

Gift-Giver

Prayer for the Gift-Giver
Ari

For all that we are given
That sets our hearts alight,
For all that we are given
That girds us for each fight,
For all that we are given
That sharper makes our sight,
For all that we are given,
We thank you, Lord of Light.

For all that we are given
That makes us weep and mourn,
For every gift that chokes us,
For every hope forlorn,
For all that we are forced to learn
That someday we will bless,
O dear Lord Frey who sees our tears,
We thank you nonetheless.

For all that we are given
That makes us reach and grow,
For all that we are given
That makes us bleed and know,
For all that makes it possible
To have much more to give,
From open heart to open hands,
You teach us how to live.

A Meal Blessing

Joshua Tenpenny

> *For all who gave of their bodies and lives for this meal,*
> *I give blessings and praise.*
> *For all who toiled to harvest and prepare this meal,*
> *I give blessings and praise.*
> *For all who share this meal with me,*
> *I give blessings and praise.*

Sometimes the meals we eat are a prayer unto themselves. Food fresh from your own garden, bread baked by hand, a holiday feast shared with friends. These clearly nourish our souls as much as our bodies, and it is easy to see the sacredness in these things. A blessing spoken at these times just affirms what was already apparent. But for most of us, most of the time, modern life obscures the sacred connection between the food in front of us and the life which was sacrificed for it. This blessing prayer is meant to be an opportunity to be mindful of how and what we eat.

First, take the opportunity to look at (or speculate about) the ingredients of what you are eating. The food we eat was all alive at some point. It can be challenging when facing a brightly colored snack cake or box of chicken nuggets, but remember that Life comes only from Life. No matter how obscure or distant the connection, all food comes from the bodies of living things. So take a moment to reflect on the fields of grain, the vegetables growing on some distant farm, the wildlife displaced and the pests killed at that farm, the livestock and the grain that fed them, the dairy cows, the laying hens, the trees full of fruit. Think about where the ingredients came from, and give thanks to the living things whose sacrifice has provided this meal. Whether the sacrifice was of their life or an offering from their body, whether it was animal or plant, give them your heartfelt blessing and praise their sacrifice.

Next, take the opportunity to think about how the food got to you in its present form. Think about the people who raised the animals and grew the vegetables, and the people who did the harvesting, butchering and packing. Think about the factory workers who process the foods, the truckers who bring it from farm to factory to store, and the business men who coordinate the whole thing. Think about who cooked the food, and who taught them how to do it. Maybe this food traveled only from your garden to your plate, making a brief detour to the sink, in no one's hands but your own. Maybe this food had a trans-continental voyage, with components coming through dozens of factories, its origin shrouded in mystery. Whatever the journey, take a moment to offer a blessing to all involved in the process and thank them for their part in bringing this nourishment to you.

Finally, take the opportunity to reflect on this meal in the context of family and community. Sharing food is one of the basic forms of social bonding. Honor the bonds of kinship and hospitality which are nourished by this meal. On a more abstract level, think about other families sitting together for dinner as you are, other harried office workers having a quick lunch at their desk like you are, other parents feeding their children as you are, other commuters eating fast food while driving like you are. Think about how this meal reflects social customs or honors family traditions. Think about how this meal connects you to others, whether they are present with you or not. Offer blessing and praise for these connections.

To give this blessing formally, you might include a brief statement about the key ingredients, people, and connections involved in the meal. For a group meal, after the person offering the prayer says each line (using "we" and "us" as appropriate), the group can reply with "Blessings and praise!" For a more participatory blessing, people in the group might suggest specific things about the meal to offer blessings and praise for. For example, someone might say, "For Aunt Mimi who taught me how to make this pie, I offer blessings and praise." to which everyone replies "Blessings and praise!"

To offer the blessing briefly and informally, just let your mind wander over each of these things as you start the meal, and say to yourself, "Blessings and praise. Blessings and praise. Blessings and praise." The point isn't to turn each meal into a research project, but to encourage mindfulness and curiosity about the process by which living things become food for us. We are part of a complex network of nourishment and obligations, and this prayer traces those threads which bind us together. Let it train you in mindfulness, helping you to see how every meal is sacred.

All the Days

Joshua Tenpenny

Hail to the Lord of the beer and the barley
Hail to the Lord of the grain grown high
For the spark of your light has remained deep inside me
All the days of my life

I give thanks for my breath and my body
I give thanks for my heart and my mind
For the spark of your light has remained deep inside me
All the days of my life

Filled with Love, I rejoice in your blessing
Filled with Love, I touch the divine
For the spark of your light has remained deep inside me
All the days of my life

Day by day, I embrace the work before me
Day by day, I walk this path of mine
For the spark of your light has remained deep inside me
All the days of my life

I see you in the sunlight and starlight
I see you in the earth and the sky
For the spark of your light has remained deep inside me
All the days of my life

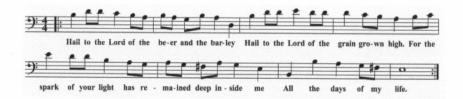

A Prayer of Gratitude to Ingvi-FreyR

K.A. Steinberg

Hail to Ingvi-Freyr
Bright one, Golden one,
Lord of Alfheim, Gullinbursti's master
Loving spouse to strong Gerd,
Dutiful son to good Njorth,
Possessor of riches that permeate
The very strands of your composition.

Good one, Protective one,
You don't fear death,
So deep is your bravery.
You sacrificed your sword for love,
Unafraid to fight at the end of the worlds barehanded.

Light one, Virtuous one,
Fair of face, Pure of heart,
Sacrificed for the grains that sustain us,
Killed and regenerated
In strength and in sorrow
So that others may live, you give yourself,
Part of you changing, dying, and reforming with each passing year

Selfless one, Faithful one,
You love with an unfettered heart
In its bright ceremonious glory.
So deep is your life force
That it itself brings life, maintains life, nourishes the fields.
The grains are your sons, the plants your daughters,
They too are sacrificed so that others may live
And they give gladly, purely, without expectation.

Wise one, Wanting one,

Stripped of your glamour you are still beautiful.
Your beauty radiates from the heart,
Its pulchritude unable to be pulled away.
Not even in death does your love falter,
For even through the very act of your death
Life springs forth.

Honorable one, Joyful one,
Lord of abundance, keener of virtuous pleasures,
So deep is your love and compassion for the world of men
That you guide us to find the ecstatic truths within ourselves,
Ever patient, often lending a hand and illuminating the way.

Guiding one, Gilded one,
Mentor, truth seeker, teacher, life-giver
He who leads by most exuberant example,
The goodness in you resonates from the core of your being;
You are fair of heart and mind.

Fair one, Fecund one
No measure of thanks could be apt repayment
For the shining glorious gifts you bring
Nor the treasures that you offer.
Your golden spirit shines like a beacon in the darkness,
Helping us to find the joy inside ourselves
And revel in life's abundances,
Guiding us towards lives well lived.
Please accept this humble prayer of gratitude
In the sincerest possible spirit of love and admiration.

Raven's Frey Altar
Raven Kaldera

Normally, my Frey altar is in the house, but occasionally it is taken outside and reassembled for a ritual, and this photo was taken during one of those occasions. The other deities are scattered about in different places—the living room, the upstairs room, etc.—but Frey insisted on remaining in our bedroom.

Perhaps it's because he was invoked during our wedding to bless our marriage; perhaps it's because he enjoys the show, regardless of whether the show is myself and my wife Bella, or myself and my partner Joshua.

The three-foot-tall woven straw man was bought at a Pagan gathering from an antiques dealer. It had been sitting around in his shop since the 1970s, and as soon as I walked by it, Frey said, "That's my votive figure. Get it." He holds my Frey necklace when I'm not wearing it, and the torc that a friend was ordered by him to give me for his regalia. The large smiling carved phallus in front of him—another remnant of the 1970s craft era—was also a gift, and has caused many people to stop and stare and ask tentatively, "Is that what I think it is?" The small straw girl is Beyla, with a beehive candle; I'm still waiting for the right Byggvir figure to arrive. His ceremonial wreath is at the bottom of the picture, and he stands between sheaves of grain and jars of corn. What you can't see are a host of small items inside the circumference of the wreath—mostly tiny pigs and phalluses and such—that have been given as votive gifts when the altar has been set out for public rites. Some are given away, but many end up on my personal Frey altar if he wants them there. The glittering golden dreamcatcher is one of those—some may cringe at the idea, but it was a gift from a sincere person of another tradition who simply wanted to honor this golden god, and Frey told me to put it with him, and there it sits. It's yet another lesson in the fact that what we think is appropriate may having nothing at all to do with what the Gods actually want.

I made the tunic for Frey out of mustard-yellow linen and embroidered the sheaves of wheat on the sleeves in metallic gold thread. It's Frey's tunic; it is only worn by Him. The necklace, on the other hand, I may wear whenever I want. It is made beads of amber and brown glass, and bears an amber pendant, a pink blown-glass phallus made by a glassblower friend, and a pig's tooth. The tooth came out of a pig's head given to us by a friend who was also an organic farmer, and had raised the pig herself. My wife took the two eyeteeth and made a pendant for each of us.

Byggvir
Seawalker

He rolls across the field, round-bellied,
Big-footed, smile wide in his face,
Clothed in brown wrinkled like the soil
That shows when the crop is cut down,
Flour whitening his face. Ears pointed, his
Alfar blood is there, but he is gnome second-
First and foremost he belongs
To the Golden One, and serves him well.
The golden grain goes into the mill,
Between the wheelstones, and he waits
Tapping his foot, humming a tune
As the oxen turn in their endless circle.
Only once a year does he go sorrowful,
Eyes filled with tears. On the day that his master
Is cut down, blood spilling in the field,
He waits, twisting hat in hand, until the
Fair body is borne away to Nerthus's hut,
And then gathers up the bloodstained kernels,
Holding them to his heart as he stumbles away.
He weeps as he mills them, tears wet circles
In the flour at his feet. The rosy powder is
Baked into cakes, and who knows what rites
That bread is devoured in? I do not ask.
Perhaps they grace the Earth-goddess's table,
Perhaps choked down by the mourning singers,
Or broken again and buried in the field.
The faithful heart gives freely of its yield,
The blood, the stone, the miller's bargain sealed.

Beyla

Seawalker

Her dress the color of the rising Sun
And floating round her round and
Buxom body, the dairymaid swings
The pail from her hand, the milk
Quick from the teat, rattles and splashes,
The gift of each spotted cow. She sings
Like a laughing gnomelike pumpkin
And the swarm comes, one by one.
They dip and kiss her sunrise hair
And lay their nectar on the elf-woman's
Tongue, in trade for her singing.
She whispers to each of them, scolds,
Encourages, asks of sisters and aunts
And the poor doomed brothers, asks
Of babies plump and pampered
In the tiny rounded rooms. Make sweetness,
Little sisters, make sweetness for our master
Who must spread joy and harmony over
Nine great worlds. Mead for his table,
Gold for his bread, he gives so much
And deserves all we can give him. Fly home,
Little sisters, and brew for a hundred days.
Her whisper carries through the flowers
That nod in the wind, the blossoms on
The crabapple tree that bloomed when
He was born, the gorse-weed and the heather.
She will have his table set with the best,
And her husband's best bread too. None shall see
Meagerness in the Golden Lord's halls,
Wherever those halls may lie. To Alfheim,
To green Vanaheim, to high blue Asgard, there are

Everywhere the frantic, buzzing hives,
Yielding to the charms of elven wives,
The joyous gift of a thousand tiny lives.

Frey at Yule
Seawalker

When I was a child and the winter holidays
Drove round with their music and lights,
If you'd said, Elves, I would have said,
Of course. Elves and gift-givers, gold balls,
Roasted nuts and the boar's head I saw
In the book on times past when it was all
Done much better than today, or so
The wistful pictures said. When I had children
I hung the boughs, put up the tree, the lights,
Made songs and cookies. When the house
Emptied of young life, years later, I gave up.
Elves, balls, trees, these were for children
Or so I thought. For sober grownups
Who are the ones to deck the halls
And take down every weary piece
Of faded glitter, sweep up all the scattered needles,
Such things quickly become burdens.
Yet somehow I did not notice when my mood
Became sour and dry, sharp as a knife's edge
When the world outside was chimes and reindeer
And inside the house was business as usual.

Frey, you simply smiled, made me notice
That one ornament in the store, that one bit
Of red-berried bough that it wouldn't hurt a bit
To break and bring inside. No trouble, that,
You said gently. See how little trouble it is.
See how little it takes to lift the darkness,
Drive it back with a candle and song—
Not sung in choir, no, merely hummed
While doing dishes and staring out over snow.
Little by little it grew, and now I go humbly

Every year to deck the house like an altar
To the Gift-Giver with the elves and gilt
Who is not Santa. You have taught me
About light in darkness, Lord who descends
And rises again. I hang your gold, I sniff
The scent of green eternal life, perhaps this year
I may even try for the boar's head,
O Lord of gentle joys who never laughs
At my stiff and foolish errors of the heart.

Yule Ritual for Frey: Silver and Gold
Raven Kaldera

This ritual commemorates Frey's yearly period in Alfheim, where he is Asgard's representative there. The position was "given to him as a tooth-gift", or so it is said. The Aesir were wise to make him the divine representative to the proud and touchy Alfar, as his frith-bringing energy is irresistible to them and they cannot find fault with him.

This rite is a public one, meant to be done in a large space. The altar is an entire table. Decorations for the altar-table can be acquired in various Christmas shops by ritual staff and participants. The table should be draped with sparkling white, like the snow at a northern Yule (even if you live in a southerly place). Set the table with lovely dishes. Some will be heaped with food, and some with decorative and symbolic items. On one half of the table, set Yule items that are colored with sparkling silver—painted and be-glittered flowers, leaves, pine cones, faux-icy branches, jeweled fruits, etc. The idea is to evoke an elfin wonderland on that side. Put out a silver bowl and a bottle of some fine clear liquor. On the other half, lay out golden items for Frey—golden ornaments, gold-sprayed wheatsheaves, gilded nuts, etc. Use your imagination. Put out a gold-colored bowl and a bottle of mead. Other props include a bell and several pieces of gold and silver thread or yarn. Each piece should be more than half the length of the table, and each gold piece should be tied to a silver piece so that they make one long strand. The gold-and-silver strands should be laid across the edges of the table, with the right color on the right side.

If there will be people present who do not drink alcohol—children, people in recovery, people with health issues, etc.—make it a matter of hospitality to have two sets of gold and silver bowls or other containers (perhaps differently shaped to tell them apart), and have a nonalcoholic clear and golden liquid on each side next to the liquor and mead. We suggest white grape juice and the clear yellow type of apple cider. When it is time to pass the drink, if there are two kinds of drink, it's easiest to designate someone to be the "cup-bearer" beforehand and walk around the circle with the two cups, so that people can choose and not feel pressured or unwelcome. If they want neither, let them know that they can kiss the cup and pass it on, or if the rite takes place outside, pour a few drops onto the ground.

Ask participants to bring small portions of food that can be given as offerings—small cakes, breads, cookies, sugared fruits, etc. Some can be given as an offering to the Alfar, and some to Frey. It's best if there are some of each, which gives a chance for people who either aren't very connected to the Alfar, or aren't very connected to Frey, to have a chance to participate. (Ideally, the large portions of food, and the messy food, go to the potluck table which is elsewhere.) Those with offerings for Frey should stand on the golden side of the table, and those with offerings for the Faery Folk should stand on the silver side of the table.

Participants can also bring gifts to exchange for each other, or if this is not practical (for instance, at an open event where not everyone knows everyone, or where people do not have a lot of money or resources) a number of small random gifts can be bought or made and placed in a basket on or near the table. Group gifting should be arranged in such a way that is the least uncomfortable for those attending. This should be a time of joy, not of shame or pressure. If anyone feels like they have not contributed enough to deserve a gift, a small chore can always be found for them to do to give back, but this should be handled as graciously as possible.

The officiant rings the bell and calls out "Hail to Frey, the Lord of Alfheim!" The people repeat it back to him. Then he says, "Hail to the ancient Alfar and their Lords and Ladies!" Again, this is repeated back. The officiant then recites:

We gather here on this day of darkness
And celebrate light in the midst of shadow.
We gather here on this day of winter
And celebrate abundance in all its forms.
We gather here in this time of difficulty
And celebrate peace and friendship
Between very different people.
Frey, our golden Lord, comes to the Elves,
Those ancient, brilliant folk of legend
Whose mystery and knowledge is renowned.
Gifts are exchanged, and webs of obligation
Are formed by the promises inherent in those gifts.

We gather here on this, the shortest day
To learn about the true nature of gifting:
That while it must be done with an open heart
And no agenda, the obligation of a gift for a gift
Is not a burden to be cast off as quickly as possible,
But a net of threads that hold us together,
That bear us up when we fall,
That remind us to be grateful
For all the folk who have gifted us,
And all the gifts unlooked-for that are yet to come.
It reminds us also that as gifts are given to us,
From other folk and from divine hands,
So must we also gift in turn, not out of duty
But out of the joy of being the hands of the Gift-Giver.

Come forth now, you who would gift the Gift-Giver,
You who would offer your gold to the Golden One,
Come forth and lay down your open hearts!

The participants on the gold side of the table come forth and lay down their gifts, saying, "We are the hands of the Gift-Giver!" If they wish, they can say what the gifts are and why they were moved to give that thing; e.g. "This is baked apple filled with cinnamon raisins, because my grandmother used to make them for us at Christmas and I want to offer a piece of that memory to Frey." The officiant says:

Come forth now, you who would gift the faery-gifters,
You who would wish blessings on the wish-granters,
Come forth and lay down your inspirations!

The participants on the silver side of the table come forth and lay down their gifts, saying, "We are the hands of the Wish-Granters!" If they wish, they can say what the gifts are and why they were moved to give that thing; e.g. "These sugared fruits reminded me of stories I read about faeries and elves when I was young." The officiant says:

On this day of abundance
We celebrate the web of obligation
That binds us together in so many ways.
Take the thread, hold it, and see to your surprise
Who stands at the other end of it.

The people on each side come and take a thread; as they pull, the threads are drawn taut across the table by folk on each side. If there are more people on one side, the difference should be made up by the officiant and other members of the ritual staff who have been briefed. The officiant says:

Two by two, you have given,
Two by two, you shall be gifted together.
Come forth and take a gift,
And may you always remember this bond.

In opposite pairs, people come to the middle still holding their ends of the thread, and receive gifts from the gift basket. When all have received gifts, the threads are collected, knotted in the middle. Each side of the bundle is pulled apart to make a giant X, which is held up by

*four people, and then laid out on the table. The officiant or another
with a strong voice galdrs the rune Gebo/Gyfu while this is being done.
Others can join in as they please. When the galdr dies down, the
officiant recites the Prayer to the Gift-Giver, either alone or as a call-
and-response. Then the officiant says:)*

The gifts have been accepted,
And frith is made once more.
Knowledge will be traded for joy,
Inspiration will be traded for fertility,
And immortality for sacrifice.
We will drink to a joyous Yule for all!

*The silver liquor is poured, some into the silver bowl by the "silver"
people, and some into the gold bowl by the "gold" people. The mead is
likewise mixed. If there is juice or other nonalcoholic drink as well, they
are mixed similarly. Then the bowls are passed around. After everyone
has drunk and toasted, the officiant repeats the "Hail Frey!" and "Hail
the Alfar!" and the people are dismissed to eat and be festive. Later,
when everyone has departed, the ritual staff takes the food outside to lay
on the earth in some safe place, and pours the remaining drink onto the
earth.*

The Boar's Head Carol (Revised)
Raven Kaldera

If you should want to cook a boar's head for a Yule Frey feast, that's a good follow-up for after the preceding ritual. Those who aren't up to cooking (or even finding) a real boar's head can make a mock one; I have seen them formed out of a small ham with a mixture of ground pork and bread crumbs molded onto it in the shape of a boar's head. The eyes were hard-boiled eggs mostly buried in the meat mix, with pupils inlaid of some round bit of vegetable. The ears were folded slices of ham extruding from the meat mixture, the bristles were bits of sweet potato, and the tusks were carved radishes added after cooking. The whole thing had been brushed with egg yolk and then baked, and arranged on a platter surrounded by other small goodies.

The boar's head was traditionally serenaded from the 15th century on, in England at least, with the original version of the following carol. We removed the Latin bits and replaced them with English, and changed the Mediterranean herbs for northern ones (*safine* is juniper berries, often used for meat spicing, and cherries are for Frey). Most of the rest of the words are the same—the "King of Bliss" reference works fine for the Golden One.

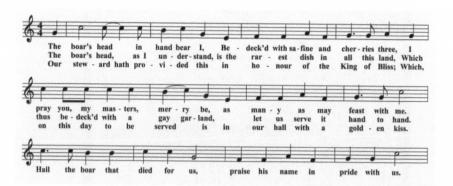

The Boar's Head Carol

The boar's head in hand bear I,
Bedeck'd with safine and cherries three,
I pray you, my masters, merry be,
As many as may feast with me.

CHORUS:
Hail the boar that died for us,
Praise his name in pride with us.

The boar's head, as I understand,
Is the rarest dish in all this land,
Which thus bedeck'd with a gay garland
Let us serve it hand to hand.

CHORUS

Our steward hath provided this
In honour of the King of Bliss;
Which, on this day to be served is
In our hall with a golden kiss.

CHORUS

Yule Recipes for a Frey Feast

Ham in Pastry Crust
Raven Kaldera

Ingredients:
1 3-pound or larger ham
Prepared mustard
Salt and pepper
A batch of the Lammas bread dough
1 egg, beaten

Preheat oven to 400 degrees and grease a baking sheet. Rub the ham with mustard, salt, and pepper. Roll out the premade dough onto a floured surface and lay the ham top-down on it. Carefully wrap the ham in the dough, sealing up the edges underneath by wetting the dough. Turn the whole thing over and put it on the baking sheet. Out of the dough scraps, make wheat stalks as in the Lammas bread recipe and apply them to the top of the crust with water. I usually arrange them in a sunburst, but you could make a sheaf over the whole top of the loaf. Prick the crust with a fork around the sides to let steam escape. Brush the whole thing with egg white and bake for an hour and a half or until the crust is golden brown. Transfer to a platter and let everyone admire it before slicing.

Pretzels

Seawalker

Ingredients:
½ cup warm water
1 ¼ tsp. active dry yeast
1 tsp. honey
¾ cup milk
1 tsp. salt
4 ½ tsp. melted butter
5 cups flour
2 tsp. salt
1 tsp. baking soda
Coarse salt crystals

Grease a baking sheet and set aside. In a large bowl, dissolve yeast and honey in warm water, let stand until foamy, around 10 minutes. Beat in the fine salt, the milk, the melted butter, and 2 cups of flour. Let stand 10 minutes, then add enough remaining flour to make a soft dough. Turn out the dough onto a floured surface and knead it for about 10 minutes, until it is smooth and elastic. Cover and let rise in a warm place for about half an hour, then punch it down. Now you make pretzels out of it—I find the easiest way is to keep dividing it in half and thirds until you have 24 pieces and then roll each piece into a long thick roll and make a pretzel. Cover pretzels and let rise for 10 minutes.

Bring a large pot of salted water to a boil and stir in baking soda. Lay the pretzels in carefully with a slotted spoon, a few at a time. Don't crowd them. When they float to the surface, scoop them out and drain them on paper towels. Put them on the baking sheet, make a few shallow angled incisions on each one, and sprinkle them with the coarse salt. Bake for 30 minutes or until lightly browned at 425 degrees.

Frey's Cakes
Tchipakkan

This is one of ever so many "shortbread-made-with-ground-nuts" cookies. Originally it was made with bitter almonds, but since those aren't usually available, we spice the flavor of sweet almonds with extra almond extract.

Ingredients:
1 cup sugar
4 cups flour
2 tsp. baking powder
1 cup butter
1 grated lemon rind
¼ pound bitter almonds (or add 3 tsp. almond extract to ¼ pound normal "sweet" ground almonds)

Mix, chill for an hour, roll into walnut-sized balls, and roll the balls in sugar. Bake on greased or lined cookie sheets for 11 minutes at 350°. Before baking, you can decorate the top with a sliced almond.

Spicy Cherry Cake
Seawalker

Ingredients:
2/3 cup butter
1 cup sugar
4 eggs
3 oz. unsweetened chocolate, grated
2/3 cup grated walnuts or blanched grated almonds
1 cup fine white breadcrumbs
1 ½ tbsp. flour
1 ¼ tsp. baking powder
1 ¼ tsp. ground cinnamon
¼ tsp. ground nutmeg
¼ tsp. ground allspice
1 tsp. finely grated orange peel
1 tsp. finely grated lemon peel
1 pound cherries, pitted

Preheat oven to 375 degrees. Butter a 10" round pan. Beat together butter and ¾ cup sugar. Beat eggs until fluffy and lemony, mix into the butter. Add chocolate, nuts, breadcrumbs, flour, baking powder, and spices and stir. Spoon into buttered pan and smooth down the surface. Arrange the cherries on the cake top and sprinkle with the remaining sugar. Bake for 45 minutes or until done; carefully turn cake out and cool. Dust with powdered sugar.

About the Editor

Joshua Tenpenny is a devoutly religious Pagan, and would be incredibly conservative if he weren't such a deviant. His spiritual affections are split between Frey, Shiva, and an assortment of love goddesses who refuse to fit neatly into his strictly polytheistic worldview. He is a massage therapist, shiatsu practitioner, and yoga teacher. He lives on the far end of a little town in Massachusetts with his partner Raven, his housemates, his fuzzy dog, and an assortment of livestock.

Photo Credits

P. 10 *English Green Man* by Richard Croft

P. 19 *Frey Statue* by Oggi

P. 27 *Wheat* by TouTouki

P. 52 *Wheat* by Shiner

P. 36 *Brassica oleracea* by Forrest and Kim Starr

P. 62 *Maypole in Ostfriesland* by Matthias Sussen

P. 65 *Joshua at the Frey Pole* by Wintersong Tashlin

P. 67 *Midsommarstang in Sweden* by Markus Bernet

P. 91 *Maypole in Trauenstein* by C.F. Wong

P. 98 *Jarmeryk* by Piotr

P. 149 *Wheat* by Mitz

P. 164 *Wheat* by Magarts

P. 172 *Wheat* by Shiner

P. 175 *Buckland Abbey Herb Garden* by Neil Kennedy

P. 222 *Marzipan Pig* by Malene Thyssen

P. 234 *Joshua* by Wintersong Tashlin

All other photos and illustrations are either public domain, or are uncredited at the request of the artist.

Reprint Credits

The following pieces previously appeared in *Gifts of the Golden God* by Sigrún Freyskona, Asphodel Press, 2007:

The Golden One by Raven Kaldera
Homestead by Raven Kaldera
Garden by Raven Kaldera
Planting A Frey Garden by Raven Kaldera
Raven's Frey Altar by Raven Kaldera
Lammas Night by Joshua Tenpenny
A Prayer of Gratitude to Ingvi-Freyr by K.A.Steinberg
Prayer to Frey, God of the Body by Michaela Macha
Gerd Meets Frey by Michaela Macha
Prayer to Frey, God of Fertility by Michaela Macha
My Fulltrui Is Frey The Bold by Michaela Macha
What Shall We Sing To Frey by Michaela Macha
Serving Gerda by Galina Krasskova
Hail The Golden God by Galina Krasskova
The Hungry Golden God by Galina Krasskova
Bringer of Light by Jon Norman

Gerda's Three Weddings previously appeared in *The Jotunbok* by Raven Kaldera, Asphodel Press, 2006.

Invocation to Frey and *Invocation to Gerda* previously appeared in *The Pagan Book Of Hours* by the Order of the Horae, Asphodel Press, 2007.

Frey's Lesson previously appeared in *Wyrdwalkers* by Raven Kaldera, Asphodel Press, 2007.

Recipe for *Frey's Pigs* and *Frey's Cakes* previously appeared in *Divine Cookies,* Asphodel Press, 2005, and *The Heathen Cookie Book,* Asphodel Press, 2010.